BUSHCRAFT

HOW TO LIVE IN JUNGLE AND BUSH

I0421846

by

"WONTOLLA"

PALMER RIVER PUBLISHING Co.
Cairns, Australia

Dedicated to C. S. SNOW

This book has been read by the General Staff (Directorate of Military Training) Allied Land Force H.Q., who agree that it provides a valuable addition to official publications on the same subject.

We were pleased to have had the opportunity of perusing the manuscript of the book entitled "Bush- craft" by "Wontolla" and this Association strongly recommends it to all Scouts, as much of the informa-tion given therein cannot but help prove invaluable to them in many of their outdoor activities.

We are confident that the book will prove extremely popular.

THE BOY SCOUTS' ASSOCIATION
New South Wales Branch.

BUSHCRAFT

How to Live in Jungle and Bush

This Edition Copyright © 2013 by
Palmer River Publishing

Cover, graphics and layout by
Palmer River Publishing

ISBN-13: 978-1484854532
ISBN-10: 1484854535

FOREWORD

I should be happy to write a Foreword introducing the contents of this little textbook at any time, because of its value to those who have discovered the extreme pleasure of an interest in Nature — whether of its wild life or its superb geological monuments.

At the present time, however, war in the Southwest Pacific areas has forced an almost unpopulated and very wild country on the interest of former city dwellers who are often ignorant of the methods of looking after them¬selves even in the Australian bush. I refer to soldiers and members of all Services, who may be faced with the jungle or bush for one reason or another, by accident or design. Field craft has thus become an essential part of the soldier's training.

"This is a war of infiltration — a war in which little packets of men, or even the individual, work, their way forward relying on their own skill." They must use their own cunning to outwit the enemy.

The man who has some knowledge of bushcraft will use the jungle and the bush to his great advantage.

I can sincerely recommend this little guide with the warning that reading must be accompanied by practice. The reader will find its exercises as fascinating and interesting as they can be useful.

W. J. DAKIN,

Professor of Zoology,
University of Sydney.

Technical Director of Camouflage,
Department of Home Security,
Canberra.

ACKNOWLEDGMENTS:

For references: The works of F.E. Williams, Mel Ward.

The encouragement of Paddy Pallin, D. R. Solomon, Allan Baker, Wilbur Morris.

To practical co-operation of Ross Carpenter, Johnnie McGruer, Peter Stewart, Bill Towers, Em Tosi, Bert Milne, Bluey Edwards, Bert Dunstone, Dick Jillett, Jim Nugent, Jack Carridge, Bill Brown.

INTRODUCTION

Around and about you in the bush are food and materials for shelter and the wherewithal for many emergencies. The true bushman if bitten by a snake and being without knife for incision or thong for ligature, will see where a flake of glass can serve him for knife, or if glass be not available a chipped quartz or jasper pebble; and for a thong will see at his very feet innumer¬able ground vines or other plants whose strength may be even greater than the piece of string or bootlace he requires for a thong. The bushman will survive where the city man would die.

The bushman can boil water when he has no billy to hang on the fire; he can make a fire when he has no matches. He can make one match light him two or three fires, and with his axe he can build him a shelter; make for himself traps, catch his food, even make his bed and his lamp and his drinking vessel. Pages in this text book and the illustrations that accompany them are offered you for the preservation of your life if you are a soldier; for your instruction if you are a bushman; for your greater comfort if you are a bush lover; and for your greater enjoyment and pleasure if you are one of the world-wide brotherhood of scouts. And if you want another good book on bushcraft, get "Bush Walking and Camping," by F. A. Pallin.,

One final admonition: Never kill unless for the pot — never chop down a green tree for a pole if there are dry poles near by — never wantonly destroy any plant or animal — study the bush, learn to read its secrets; watch a mason fly building and go to the ant for another lesson and you'll realise that the bush is your friend.

Contents

Foreword   i

Acknowledgments: ii

Introduction   iii

Chapter 1 - Huts, knots and
rope-making   1

Chapter 2 - Traps and snares   17

Chapter 3 - Sources of water
and water treatment   33

Chapter 4 - Edible plants, animals,
birds and insects   42

Chapter 5 - Firelighting, camp
accessories, cooking
and tools   56

Chapter 6 - Water travel   70

Chapter 7 - Direction finding
and time   81

CHAPTER 1
Huts, Knots and Rope-making

1   *Thatch Huts. General.*

2   *Small Huts.*

3   *Circular Hut.*

4   *Hut.*

5   *Knots, lashings, bindings.*

6   *Thatching.*

7   *Log Cabins.*

8   *Ropes and natural materials.*

9   *Laying up for cords and ropes and plaits.*

10   *Lianas, monkey ropes.*

HUTS AND SHELTERS

The making of shelters in the bush is an easy matter when you know how. The type of shelter depends on the length of time you intend to occupy it, the material available and the number of people it has to shelter. You can build a thatch hut, a bark humpy or a log cabin, depending entirely upon the requirements of your party and the materials available to your hands. In none of these structures are man-made materials necessary and the only tools required are a couple of pairs of hands and either a good knife or a tomahawk or axe.

1.   THATCH HUTS

The structure can be either made up on living trees or by the use of forked poles. There are three main types of design: the lean-to, the circular and the long hut.

Circular hut, eighteen feet in diameter, twelve-feet peak, built by five men in one day.

(Drawn from actual photograph.)

2.   LEAN-TO HUT

The lean-to hut is very simple and quick to erect.

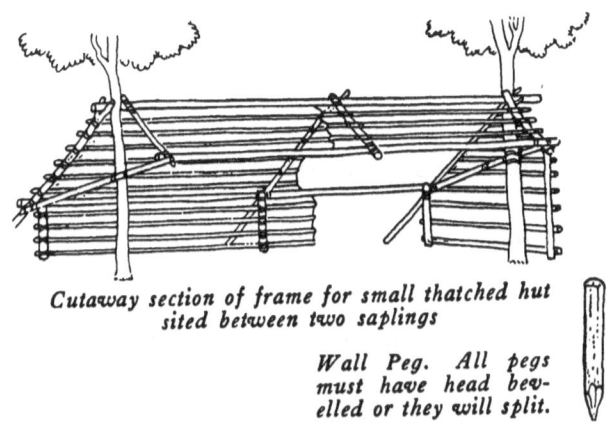

Cutaway section of frame for small thatched hut sited between two saplings

Wall Peg. All pegs must have head bevelled or they will split.

The ridge pole is raised against the trees by means of the two end forked poles to the required height. Seven to eight feet is generally sufficient.

The end forked poles should be at an angle of not less than 45 deg. If the span of ridge is more than 10 to 12ft., it is advisable to put in another forked pole about half way along.

On to the end forked poles lash a crossbar and lash it again to the upright tree. This cross bar has lashed to its front end a pole connecting and lashed to the ridge, and also a front eaves pole and the thatching battens.

Thatching battens are also lashed on to the two rear forks. The distance apart for the thatching battens varies; it may be anything from 6 to 18in., depending on the thatching material being used. A general guide is that battens should be distant about one-fourth of the average length of the thatching material.

An upright which may be a light fork is secured under the front end poles to the front eave pole. Wall thatch battens are lashed from the rear forked poles horizontally to this upright. Wall pegs are driven in along the rear at whatever is the required wall height and to these wall pegs thatching battens are also lashed.

Forked poles should be about 3 to 4in. – thatching battens from 1 1/2 to 3in. Ridge pole about 2 to 4in.

Use dry timber or dead timber wherever possible. It is lighter to handle and its use preserves the bush. When making wall pegs bevel off the head – they will drive into the ground without splitting.

3. CIRCULAR HUT

Use four forked poles, the forks of which lock together at the top. These poles should be about 45 deg. from the ground.

Thatched hut, twelve feet in diameter, erected by two men in one day.
(Drawn from actual photograph.)

To each of these four interlocking forked poles (which roughly form a pyramid) two poles are lashed just below the fork. These poles roughly divide the area between the forked poles into sections of 30 deg., and their base on the ground forms a rough circle, of which the inter¬locking point of the four poles is the centre.

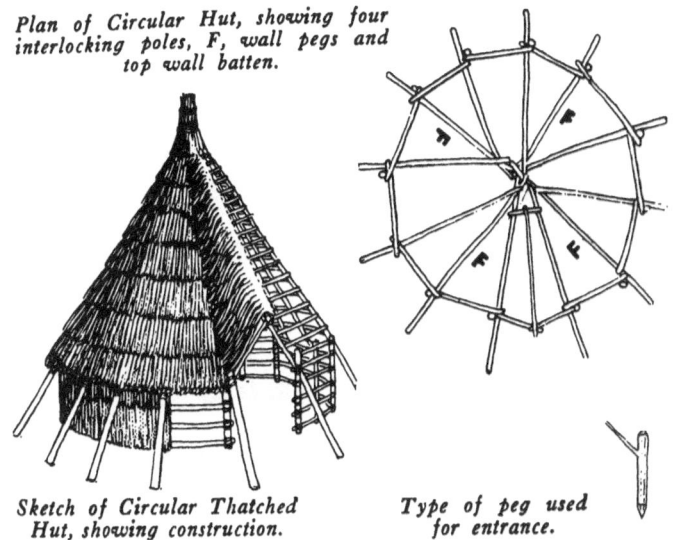

Plan of Circular Hut, showing four interlocking poles, F, wall pegs and top wall batten.

Sketch of Circular Thatched Hut, showing construction.

Type of peg used for entrance.

At the required wall height, wall pegs are driven in alongside these twelve poles and lashed to them, leaving an opening between one section where required for entrance. The wall pegs here can be about 6 to 7ft. high, cut from two forks, with the side arms crossing about 7ft. from the ground. These two side arms are lashed together and a ridge pole can be lashed from them to the peak.

The thatching battens are lashed horizontally and the whole structure is thatched.

The four forked poles can be from 3 to 6in. diameter —the intermediate poles about 3 to 4in. diameter, and thatching battens from 1 to 2in. diameter. Such a hut could be from 12 to 24ft. diameter, but it is necessary to preserve the 45 deg. slope. The entrance structure can be simplified if required. To provide light inside a drop frame section can be made if required, that is, secured like a hinge by lashings at the top to lift outwards.

Refinements such as this can be left to the builders' choice.

4.   LONG HUT

Hut, sixty feet long, twenty feet wide, by sixteen feet high, built by five men in eight days.

(Drawn from actual photograph.)

The end portion of the structure is basically the same as one-half section of the round hut.

The length can be extended to any required distance by prolonging the ridge pole and using additional sup¬porting fork poles. If the ridge is extended and in two or more lengths, these should be lashed together, and it is advisable to notch the ridge so it will sit snugly in the interlocking forks.

Wall, pegs are driven in at a convenient wall height and thatching battens are lashed down. Refinements such as "lift up" sections for light and ventilation can be added if required.

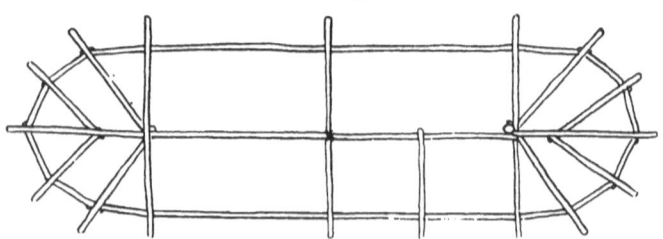

Plan of long hut, showing position of end interlocking forked poles and ridge pole.

5.   KNOTS, LASHINGS AND BINDINGS

In all hut buildings and bush work it may be necessary to use only natural materials; therefore it is important to know knots, lashings and bindings.

KNOTS

THUMB KNOT
To make a stop on a rope to prevent end from fraying or to prevent it slipping through a sheave.

FIGURE EIGHT
Use as for a thumb knot, but easier to untie.

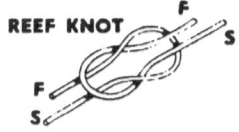

REEF KNOT
To join two ropes of equal thickness.

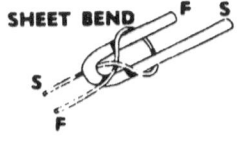

SHEET BEND
To join or bend two ropes of unequal thickness together. The thicker rope is the bend.

DOUBLE SHEET BEND
As above, with greater security; also useful for joining wet ropes.

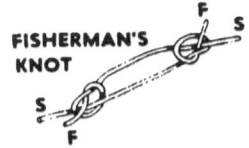

FISHERMAN'S KNOT
For joining two springy materials together; suitable for wire, fishing gut or vines. Two thumb knots (one on each rope), pulled tight. The knots lock together.

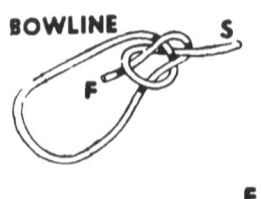

BOWLINE
To form a loop on a rope that will not slip.

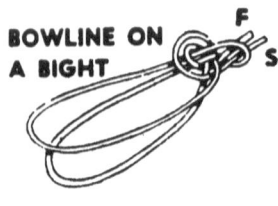

BOWLINE ON A BIGHT
To make a double loop on a rope that will not slip.

TIMBER HITCH
For holding timber or logs, etc.; also a good starting knot for lash¬ings where the strain keeps the cord tight.

CLOVE HITCH
For securing a rope to a spar— this hitch, if pulled taut, will not slip up or down on a smooth surface. Useful start for lashings.

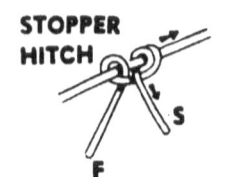

STOPPER HITCH
To fasten one rope to another rope on which there is already a strain —when the hitch is pulled tight the attached rope will not slip and the tension on the main rope can be taken on the attached rope.

NOTE –   *F means the free end of the rope.*
               S means the standing or secured end.

LASHINGS

SQUARE LASHING — To join poles at right angles.

 Start with a timber hitch or a clove hitch below cross bar. If using a timber hitch see that the pull is straight through the eye and not back from it. Pulling back will cut the lashing material.

 Put lashing material tightly around upright and cross bar about four complete times.

 Frapping turns — make about two or three frapping turns. These pull the lashing taut and secure. Secure end of frapping turns either by half-hitches or by passing under lashing and half-hitches over lashing itself.

SHEER LASHING — To join two poles end to end.

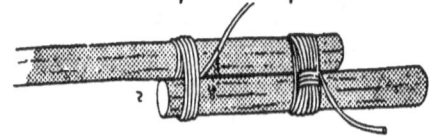

Start with a clove hitch or timber hitch, lash tightly around the two spars four to six times. Pass free end under lashings and draw tightly two or three times. Secure by passing it through itself, as in 2.

There should be at least two lashings if spars are being joined together.

DIAGONAL LASHING — For bracing or joining spars at irregular angles.

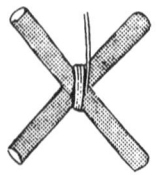

Start with a timber hitch or a clove hitch and take about three or four full turns vertically.

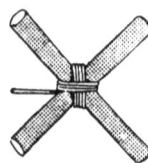

Pass rope under top spar and make about three or four full turns horizontally.

Take two or three frapping turns and either secure by two halfhitches on pole or by passing the end between the lashing and the pole and use half-hitches on the lashing.

BINDING — To prevent rope from fraying, or to bind on material.

Binding — turn one end down and bend over; after 15 or 20 turns fold back into loop and bind free end under three or four turns. Put end of binding through loop, and pull through by pulling free end of loop. Pull binding in right under the last turns and cut off.

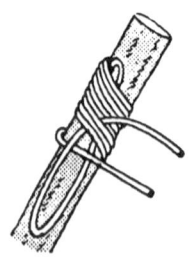

6.   THATCHING

Materials suitable for thatching include long grass, reeds, palm leaf, Xanthorrhoea (Grass Tree, Blackboy or Bullrush), bracken or ferns, or branches of bushes.

MATERIAL	TREATMENT
Grass reeds, etc.	Pull, or if cut dry, it is advisable to damp down to make less brittle.
Ferns or bracken	Pull or cut green—use full length of stalk. A thick thatch is required.
Palm .... Xanthorrhoea .... (Grass Tree, Blackboy)	If used green no special treatment; if dry, damp down to remove brittleness.
Branches and bushes	Use green bushes; do not chop down indiscriminately —thin out rather than denude an area. Branches are not a good material if others listed above available.

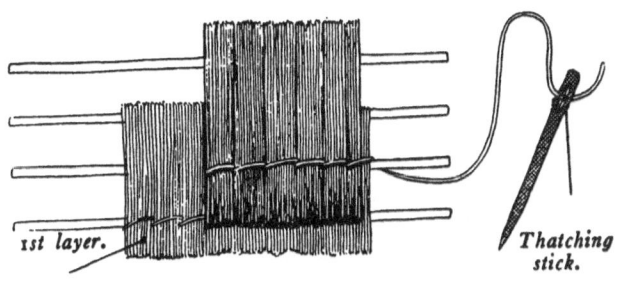

1st layer.

Thatching stick.

Showing Sequence of Thatching.

Stitch at bottom of first thatch on lowest thatching batten.

Second layer of thatch, the ends of which must cover stitching and first or bottom layer of thatch, and stitching of second layer goes right through layers

11

underneath, securing them to thatching bottom.

Thatching stick. Fire hardened at point, hole bored at end. Rub stick smooth on a piece of rock — length about 12in. to 18in., and about 3in. diameter.

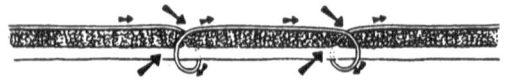

Showing Direction of Sewing Thread in Thatching.

Lay grass, rushes or branches or palm leaves with butts to¬wards roof, sew down along bottom batten. Repeat with second layer of thatch, sewing it on to the second batten. The loose ends of this layer must overlap the sewing of the lower layer.

To avoid holes where the sewing may tend to bunch the thatch together, pass the needle through the thatch at the angle indicated by the arrow and push thatch over crossing of stitches — pull stitching tight after each stitch.

RIDGE THATCH

Top or ridge thatch curls right over ridge pole, as is shown on ridge pole and on thatching battens first below ridge. The ends overhang the stitching of the top layer of thatch.

End view of ridge thatch and ridge pole at top in centre.

A well thatched hut, securely lashed, should still be serviceable after 12 months to three or four years. Very little maintenance is required. The fire risk is fairly considerable. If green or unseasoned material is used for construction, sewing and lashings should be tightened a few days after completion. If seasoned materials are used they should be stretched before use.

Thatched huts are completely rain proof and wind proof. They are cool in hot weather and warm in cold weather. If they are to be occupied in cold climate, a good plan is to leave a smoke hole in the roof and to warm them with a fire in a small stone fireplace. (See Chap. 5.)

7.   LOG CABINS

Method of halving logs for secure join.

The method of construction is simply the scarfing or halving of logs. This method, while quite useful for a permanent struc¬ture, is not entirely satisfactory in Australia, because it involves a considerable wastage of timber and because of the ravages of white ants. If the logs are poisoned with arsenic it would probably be satisfactory.

8.   ROPE MAKING AND PLAITING

Ropes, cords, plaits and thongs and ties for all sorts of purposes lie ready to your hand in the bush. From materials as wide apart as grass and bark you can make rope of any length and any strength. From innumerable ground vines you can secure material ready made for lashings and thongs. Many of these native plants are more supple if heated. The sap "steams" them.

MATERIAL	PREPARATIONS FOR USE	USE
Long grass and reeds	Plait or twist and lay	Suitable for rope for lashing and bindings.
Giant Lily (Doryanthes) Outside leaves only	Heat over fire. Tear off from centre rib	Unplaited, use for sewing thatch, for light bindings and lashings.
	Centre rib. Bash butt end to soften and thin off, tie together with sheet bend and pull tight	Plaited or laid may be used for rope for all purposes.

13

MATERIAL	PREPARATIONS FOR USE	USE
Settlers' Twine (Gymnostachys Anceps)	Separate fibres and lay up for thin cord for lines for fishing or snares .... Bash butts for making rope	Very tough for lashings and bindings. For lashings and bindings. May be plaited for rope, etc. Use four plait for round rope. As a sewing material for thatching or as a binding material.
Green wattle bark	Heat over fire	Plait strips for binders or for lashings.
Stringy bark or fibrous inner bark of many of the eucalypts	Shred into long strips Teased into fibres	Laid up into strands and re-laid in lays and again re-laid for rope.
Vines	Generally more supple if heat treated	For sewings, lashings and snares, etc.

9.   ROPE MAKING

To lay up rope use any material with a long and strong fibre. Gather up fibres into long untwisted strands each of even thickness; each of these strands is twisted clock¬wise and layer places or lays each of these twisted strands (called lays), so that a cord of even twist and thickness is built up. Note that the fibres go longwise along the direction of the rope to make rope; the twisted cords are again twisted and built up into rope. Laying up rope requires three or four people: one for each cord and one to lay.

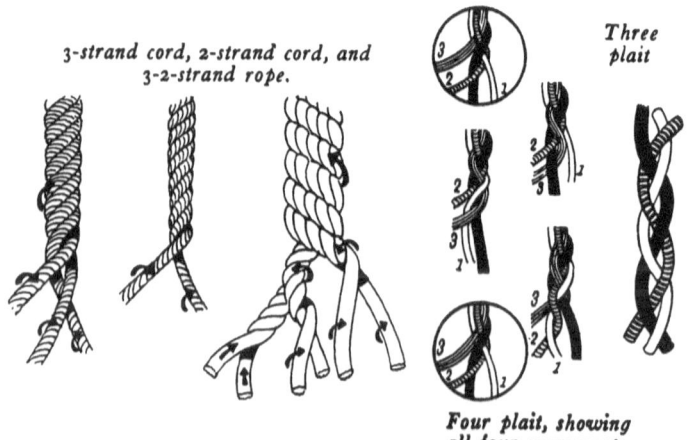

3-strand cord, 2-strand cord, and 3-2-strand rope.

Three plait

Four plait, showing all four movements.

In using bark it is advisable, if very good quality, strong rope is required, to use only the inner strips, which are stronger and longer in grain—using bark fresh from the green tree is best, but bark from dead trees is quite satisfactory and quite strong.

If making thick cable, say 2 to 4in. diameter, the only satisfactory way is to build up from strands to cords and to ropes and to relay these ropes into thick cables. This takes time, but the cables so made will be about as strong as a coir rope.

BUSH ROPE-MAKER

A bush rope-maker can be easily constructed by arranging a series of wire, or wooden cranks, connected by a crankshaft.

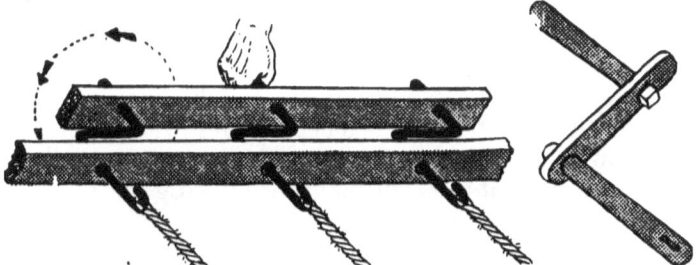

A simple method of twisting strands is by these cranks made of either wire or wood. The strands are laid together by a single crank at the opposite end to these cranks.

CORD

While the inner bark from stringy bark is quite good for fishing lines and fine cord for snares, the fibre from Settlers' Twine (Gymnostachys Anceps) will make a stronger line. The surplus green matter can be removed from Settlers' Twine by soaking for a few days in water. Settlers' Twine is found throughout the whole of Eastern Australia and the Islands. It grows just above the creeks and water courses and the leaf attains a length of from four to seven or eight feet. Many other long fibred materials are eminently suitable—experiment and find them out for yourself.

PLAITING

Four (4) plait or lariat plait will give a good round cord if a flat material is used, or if a round material is used the finished plait will be square. This is a very good plait for nooses and for thongs, etc. Take top strand, pass over two and turn back under the second. See diagrams of four stages.

Three (3) plait, suitable for fairly short fibred material and makes a quick job. Plaiting for lashing is much easier than laying up cord—keep the grass or plaiting material fed in at irregular intervals. This helps make a stronger plait. Advantage—plaiting can be easily done by one man.

10.   LIANAS AND VINES

Thick lianas (3 to 4in. diameter) grow in all the scrubs and jungles. These are of immense tensile strength. They frequently branch and it has been found practicable (for bridging and other purposes where great strength is required) to plait these thinner growths together.

This also applies to small ground vines which, when plaited, give increased strength without loss of flexibility.

TABLE OF STRENGTHS	
3 lay rope of 1in. diameter	
Material	Breaking Strain
Stringy Bark	550 lbs.
Grass	448 lbs.
Palm Fibre	672 lbs.
Settlers' Twine	2,016 lbs.
Liana	530 lbs.

CHAPTER 2
Traps and Snares

1.   General ground noose snare for all animals and birds.

2.   Ground noose snare (variation), animals.

3.   Vertical noose snare for large animals.

4.   Tree snare for tree climbing animals.

5.   Log fall trap for ground feeding animals.

6.   Log fall trap for trapping animals alive.

7.   Box trap for small animals.

8.   Log weighted platform trap for pig, wallaby and other small animals.

9.   Log fall from tree for man killing or large animals.

10.   Bow and arrow for man killing or large animals.

11.   Slap spear for man killing or large animals.

12.   Pitfall for large heavy animals.

13.   Bird traps, general.

14.   Rat traps for ducks, geese and waterfowl.

15.   Fish traps – weir type.

16.   Noose and floating stick for surface feeding fish.

17.   Vertical stick or toggle for deep water fish.

18.   Rock pool fish trap.

19.   Sea eels, luring with cungevoi.

20.   Rock and sea crabs, at night.

21.   Yabbies and fresh water fish.

Successful trapping depends on a knowledge of the habits of the animals for which one is setting the trap. It is important that the successful trapper be able to read ground signs or tracks—these can always be found in the soft ground near water. It is necessary to know what time the animals come in to drink, and to note in one's passage through bush or scrub where their tracks (or paths) are, because on these observations will depend the type of trap to be set. It is also important to remember that all animals have an acute sense of smell, and that to them the most dangerous of all smells is that of their greatest enemy, MAN. If you set a trap and leave your man scent on it, you will be indeed for¬tunate if you catch anything—you must get rid of the man scent, which you can do if you rub your hand with some strong-smelling herbage (if the animal is herbaceous) or with freshly killed meat and blood (if the animal is carnivorous). Incidentally, birds and reptiles do not seem to be as sensitive to scent as an animal or fish.

There are three lures that are worth while to remember —these are aniseed for animals and oil of rhodiun for fish. Almost all animals will come for the aniseed lure, while the lightest touch of oil of rhodiun will bring fish to your line. It is advisable to use the oil of rhodiun on the bait only, as some fish, such as leather-jackets, will bite clean through the line if it carries the lure. The third lure is the urine from the bladder of a female on heat. This will attract males.

Salt is an excellent lure or on a bait for animals. Animal traps may be roughly divided into four types: snares (using the noose), traps using weighted logs, etc., pitfalls, and missile throwers. The type of trap set depends partly on the animal to be trapped, partly on the materials locally available, and partly on the site of the trap.

1.   GROUND SNARE

Noose snare for small animals or birds.

Snare, either baited or set in the path of the animal. The size, snare and strength of setting depend on the animal to be caught.

A tree or sapling A is bent over and at its end a stout cord is secured, B. This cord is tied to a toggle stick C, which is held under a cross stick E, lying under two forked sticks F, F. The upward tension of the bent sapling A is resisted by the cord B through the toggle stick C being under the cross stick E. The toggle stick (under cross stick E) presses against the trigger D, which is pushing at its farther end against an anchor stick. The noose from the cord B lies beneath the trigger so that any touch on the trigger frees the trigger stick. The sapling springs up and the noose tightens around the neck or leg or body of the animal.

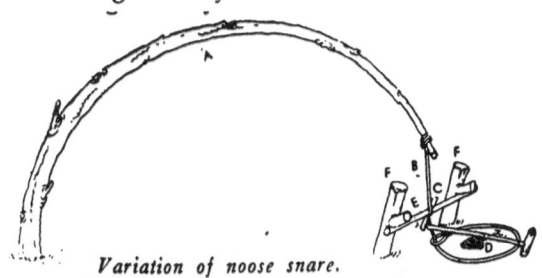

Variation of noose snare.

2.   This is a variation of the above trap. The cross stick E lies beneath two upward forked sticks F, or in two

19

niches in the two sticks F, and the trigger is a thin stick from the toggle stick C to a securing peg in the ground. The noose and bait lies beneath the trigger stick. Any disturbance of the trigger will release the snare.

Noose snare for large animals.

This is a snare suitable for setting in an animal track or path. The sapling A is bent down and a tie B is fastened to a stick C, the end of which passes under the cross bar D, and the bottom end of which presses against a loose stick E. From the sapling A the rope with the noose comes and is loosely tied to D and the two uprights F, F.

The animal in passing along its path or in grazing disturbs either C or E, thus releasing the tension and causing the noose to swing upwards.

In setting this snare, which is very suitable for such animals as deer, buffalo, etc., as well as wallaby and 'roo, it is advisable, if it is being set in an animal path, to pile branches, etc., on either side of the path and so force the animal along the pad. Even if it is suspicious it will then go forward to the trap.

If this trap is being set in the open, a light stockade of sticks or piles of brushwood should be put on the inside of the trap and in this the bait should be placed. The animal will nose around until it comes to the opening into the trap.

Several variations of these types of snares can be improvised.

4.   SNARE FOR TREE-CLIMBING ANIMALS

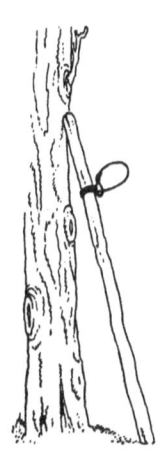 The tree trunk is examined for marks to see which trees the animal is in the habit of climbing. Fresh claw marks are the clue. Securely place a green, 8 or 10ft. sapling against the leaning side of the tree (if any) and on this, about four to five feet from the ground, place a noose (preferably of wire), so that the animal climbing up the sapling will put his head through the noose; in con¬tinuing his climb, the noose will tighten on his neck and, in struggling against it, he will fall and is strangled. Obviously one end of the noose must be securely fixed to the sapling.

NOTE: Most tree-climbing animals will become alarmed if the butt of the tree is heavily hit at frequent intervals with the back of axe or other heavy, jarring weight. Opossums, squirrels and tree-climbing kan¬garoos will climb down the trunk in daylight till about four feet from the ground, where they may be fairly easily killed.

5.   FALLING TRAP for ground-feeding animals such as pig, bandicoot, etc.

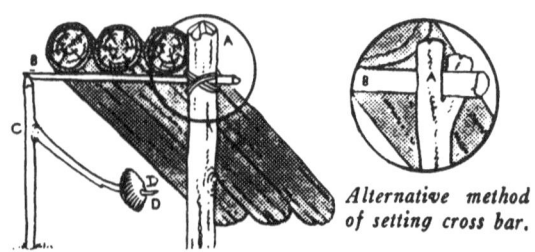

A stick A (or a forked stick) is driven securely in the ground. To this is lashed loosely a cross stick B, having its farther end cut at about 45 deg. with a clean axe cut. This cross stick is supported at this farther end by a bait stick C-D, pointed at the top end, and this point rests on the oblique cut on B. On top of B two or three heavy logs are rested, their farther ends being on the ground. The animal disturbs the bait at D, which turns the bait stick C, which slides from under the oblique cut on B, and the logs fall immediately, crushing the animal. This trap can be set very sensitively, depending on the angle at which C comes on to the cut on B. The stick C-D is merely a widely angled forked stick reversed. It is advisable to set the bottom end on a chip of wood or stone to prevent the logs driving it into the earth and thus reducing the sensitivity of the trap.

6. TO CATCH ANIMALS ALIVE

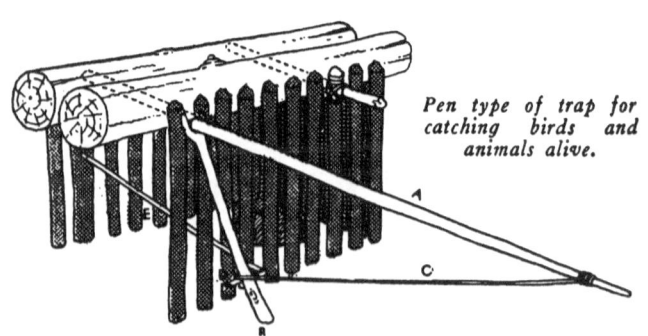

Pen type of trap for catching birds and animals alive.

The foregoing trap can be repeated with a

22

stockade built around the sides and rear end and with the same method of release by the bait stick. An alternative to this is shown opposite – the top logs are raised and secured at the rear end of a small strong stockade, at the outside or approach end the logs are held up by means of a long stick A, which passes beneath the logs and over the crutch of a strong fork stick B; to the farther end of this stick A is fastened a stout cord C, secured to a short toggle stick D, against which the opposite end of the trigger or bait stick E presses, having its farther end pressing against one of the bars of the stockade.

The bait is inside the stockade and either tied on to or beyond the trigger stick E. The animal, on entering the trap to get the bait, disturbs the trigger stick, releasing the toggle and allowing the heavy logs to fall with the inward end of the bar A. The logs being raised at the farther end of the stockade form a pen in which the animal is secured.

7. **A PORTABLE BOX TRAP** for catching small animals alive may be made from a case in which a slide door A is fitted, riding in two slides B, B.

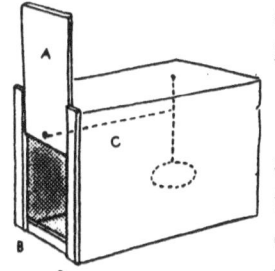

The door is held up by a wire or rod C, which passes through a hole cut in the bottom of the door, the other end of which is fastened to a bait stick a few inches below the pivot point on the roof – on the animal pushing at the bait on the bait stick, the rod C is withdrawn and the door drops shut.

8.   FALLING TRAP

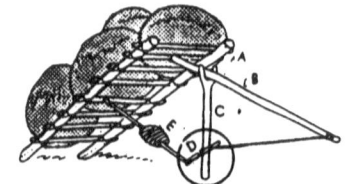 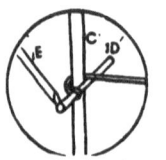

Detail of release.

Platform trap for killing small strong animals.

A killer for pig or wallaby or other small animals can be made as follows: Platform A, weighted with heavy stones, is made from two saplings and light sticks lashed on – this is kept elevated at one end by a lever stick B passing over the crutch of a forked stick C. At the farther end of the lever stick a cord is fixed, the other end of which is secured to a toggle D which passes

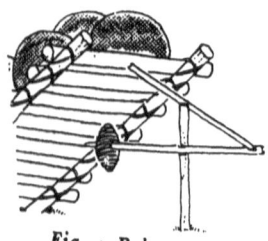

Fig. 4 Release.

around the forked stick C. The toggle tension is kept secure by a bait stick E, which is kept suspended by the pressure of the toggle stick at one end and at the other presses against the underside of the platform A. When the animal disturbs the bait stick the toggle is released and the lever stick B allows the weighted platform to fall on the animal beneath.

Alternative release for trap is this figure 4 release. Bait stick is nicked to hold against upright.

9.   SUSPENDED LOG

A killer for big animals may be made by a suspended log in a tree over a path.

24

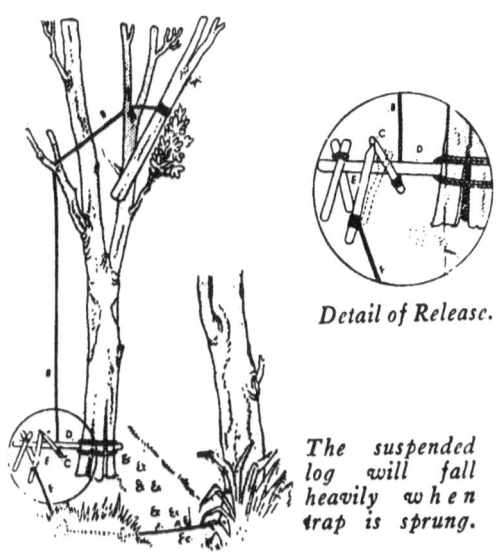

Detail of Release.

The suspended log will fall heavily when trap is sprung.

This can also be used as a man-killer trap to guard paths, etc., to outposts. The log A is hoisted up to the tree crutch and the rope B passes down the rear side of the tree and is secured to a toggle stick C which is on the lower side of a cross stick D. The toggle stick is prevented from slipping under the cross bar D by a trigger stick E, to which is connected the trip cord F. When the trip cord is touched the trigger stick E is released from the engagement with the toggle and the rope is released, allowing the log to fall on the animal. The trip (or trips, if two are used) should be about 4 to 6ft. on either side of where the log will fall (rate of fall is 26ft. per second). Sufficient distance should be allowed to permit the forward movement of the animal to coincide with the rate of log fall. This trap can be made safe when required by putting a forked stick under C, as indicated by dotted line.

NOTE: This trap is a man-killer and dangerous.

11.   BOW TRAP

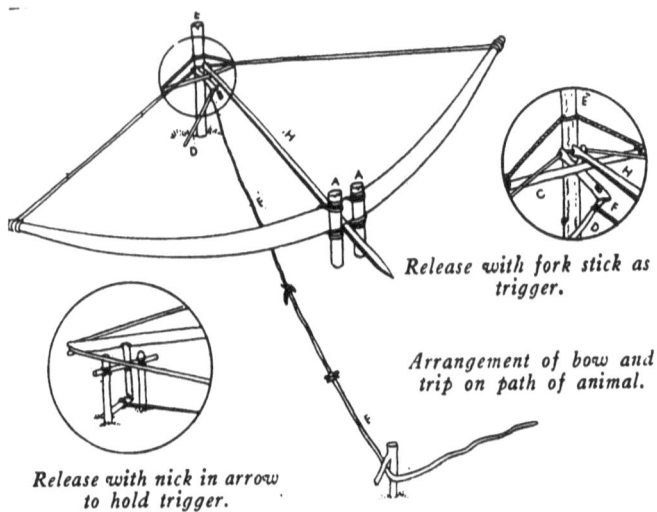

Release with fork stick as trigger.

Arrangement of bow and trip on path of animal.

Release with nick in arrow to hold trigger.

If no trees are available, another killer for man or animal is the bow. Using a long length (10-12ft.) of bamboo, myrtle or other suitable wood, the bow is roughly fashioned and secured by lashings to two up¬right pegs A, A. The thong is secured, when the bow is bent by. a forked stick B, over tip of the forked end of which the thong passes, leaving a small space between the thong and the bottom of the fork.

The forked stick B is kept back by passing behind a cross stick C, secured by ties to a peg E, firmly driven into the ground. The forked stick is retained against the tension of the bow by a trigger stick D, to which is attached the trip cord F.

Any man or animal breaking or touching the trip cord F at path will release B and allow the arrow H (which is lying with the notch in the fork of B and the head through the two sticks A, A) to fly forward.

NOTE: This and the preceding traps are exceedingly dangerous to man and will kill. By putting a forked stick without a trip in place of the trigger stick, these two traps can be made safe if and when required.

11. SLAPPING SPEAR OR THROWER

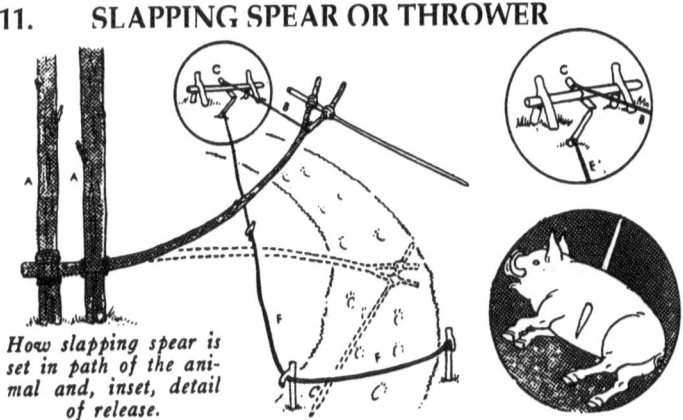

How slapping spear is set in path of the animal and, inset, detail of release.

A long springy sapling is lashed as shown to two trees A, A, and is bent back and held in position by a strong cord B, to which is secured a toggle stick C, the bottom end of which bears on a trigger stick, to which is attached the trip cord F.

To the far end of the bent sapling a spear of hardened, sharpened wood is lashed. Any animal disturbing the trip F releases the bent sapling and the spear, which sweeps around, impaling the animal. A variation of this may be made, whereby the bent sapling has at its farther end either a stone, or a loose spear. By provision of a "stop" rope the return spring of the sapling is checked and the spear or stone is thrown forward (and upward if the sapling is bent downward).

12. PIT OR DEAD FALL

A pit is dug in the ground and in it are driven

sharpened stakes, pointed end uppermost; the top is covered with bark slabs, brush and leaves to conceal the

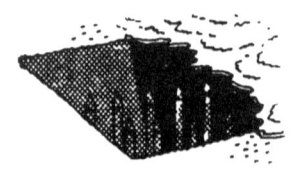 presence of the dead fall. The animal on rushing along the track breaks through the light cover and is impaled. This is not a very effective trap unless sited in a very suitable position or unless the animal is driven on to the dead fall.

13.   BIRD SNARES

Some of the foregoing are eminently suitable as bird traps, depending, of course, on the birds one is trying to trap. If set for birds they should be set near water or near feed and baited accordingly. For example: No. 1, if baited with grain or seeds and set near a pigeon-feeding area, will undoubtedly secure a pigeon, while the same trap, baited with a newly killed frog and set on the edge of water frequented by wild fowl, will secure a wild duck or goose.

In general, the most effective bird snare is simply a noose, or better, an area set with nooses; if setting for pigeons, set where they come for water and set many nooses – the fact that one bird is entangled will bring other birds to its assistance. Whereas if setting for scrub turkeys, set nooses around the feeding areas or hatching mound; or if setting for duck, set on logs out of the water where ducks go to rest and sun themselves.

Obviously, if the ground is baited, more birds will be attracted and more birds caught.

For parrots, etc., a stick with many fine nooses placed in the trees they frequent will suggest itself to them as a perch—one bird entangled and crying out will attract others, who will in turn ensnare themselves.

14.   WILD DUCK AND GEESE

Bait a rat trap with a green frog and float it on a board into the water. The board should be secured to the shore. The rat trap will invariably catch and kill your duck or goose for you.

15.   FISH TRAPS

The conventional net or wire mesh fish trap with one tunnel-shaped entrance is known to everyone, but the principle of the native fish trap may be new to some.

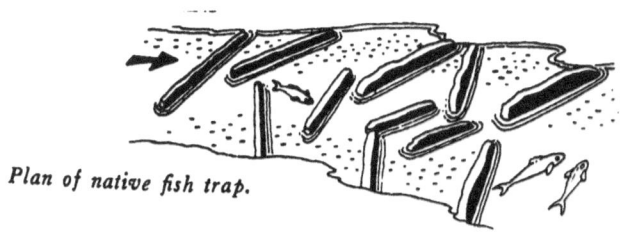

Plan of native fish trap.

The direction of flow in the diagram is illustrated by the arrow. A number of artificial angle weirs are put in the stream, having gaps and pockets. In the pockets the fish are trapped. These fish traps are easily constructed in any tidal stream at low tide. The fish travel upstream, feeding on the rising tide, and are trapped in the ebbing tide. The walls of the weirs, which may be log or stone, should be 18in. to 2ft. high if the tide rise is considerable, but will be quite effective if only 6in. to 8in.

16.   SURFACE FEEDING SEA FISH

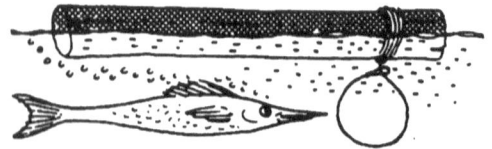

Noose snare for surface fish.

A number of light wooden sticks to which is attached a fine noose on the underside are floated out. These lie on the surface of the water. The surface feeding fish, such as garfish and long toms, lie for shelter beneath any debris on the water and naturally lie under the sticks—in darting out to get their prey, they pass through the noose, which either gets them in the fins or through the tail. The surf returns the sticks and fish (when exhausted) to the beach.

17.   FLOAT STICK

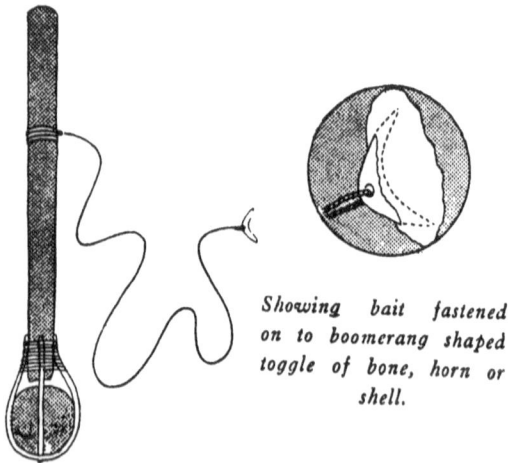

Showing bait fastened on to boomerang shaped toggle of bone, horn or shell.

An alternative, which would have application to rivers, consists of an upright stick, weighted at one end, to which is attached a few yards of line and either a hook or a toggle (as illustrated at the farther end). The hook (or toggle) is baited and the constant straining of the hooked fish against the drag of the stick will soon exhaust it. The action of the toggle is that the fish snap at the bait and the toggle prevents it from closing its mouth— it struggles against the toggle and is quickly exhausted and drowned. Both these methods of fishing are success¬fully used throughout the Pacific. Fish hooks can be improvised from strong thorns, leaving a thin portion of the stem attached as a shank.

18.   ROCK POOLS

Another method of getting good hauls of fish without fishing gear is to select a good shallow rock pool which will be covered at high tide. Burley it with bait such as crushed up pippies, cungevoi, etc., and build up a low rock wall with one opening and about half ebb tide at night close up the opening with stones previously laid close by. The fish will be trapped inside and ready for your daylight raid.

19.   SEA EELS

Sea eels can be lured like sand worms, by washing a piece of cungevoi at the edge of rocks where sea kelp is growing. The eels will come into shallow water after the bait and may be easily speared by hand or crushed with a heavy stone.

20.   ROCK AND SEA CRABS

Rock and sea crabs may be lured to light at night. This is easily the quickest way to catch a good meal of crab. All salt water crabs, except those brightly coloured, are edible. Land crabs may be regarded as poisonous.

21.   FRESH WATER FISH AND EELS

Fresh water fish and eels may be caught by the conventional methods. Yabbies, or fresh water crayfish, may be lured by meat tied to a piece of cord or string, or may be caught in a small mesh fish trap.

CHAPTER 3
Sources of Water and Water Treatment

1   *Water in arid regions and water trees.*

2   *To find water roots.*

3   *Water yielding herbage.*

4   *Water indicators.*

5   *Finches.*

6   *Pigeons and doves.*

7   *Parrots and cockatoos.*

8   *Hornets and bees.*

9   *Animals.*

10   *Dew.*

11   *Native wells and storage reservoirs.*

12   *Creek beds.*

13   *Sea shore sweet water supplies.*

14   *Water from sea fish.*

15   *Water purifying.*

1. WATER IN ARID REGIONS AND WATER TREES

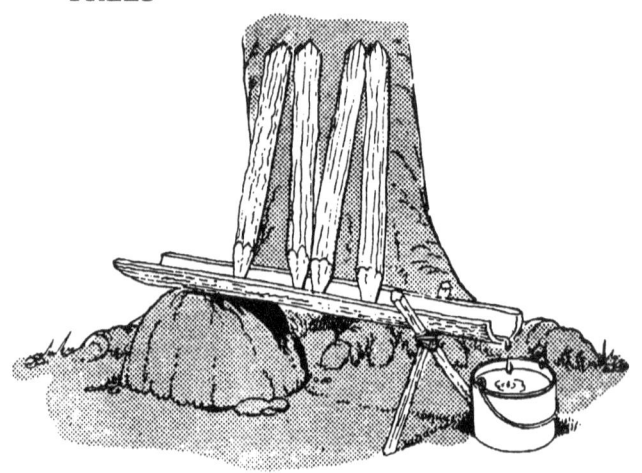

Water being collected from vines in a bark trough.

Sweet water may be obtained from many sources other than wells and streams.

In scrub country (true rain forest), abundant supplies of sweet water can be got from the various vines or Lianas, particularly one which in the structure of the stalk and leaf is like a climbing bamboo.

In dry parts of Australia the roots of almost all trees can be absolutely relied on to yield sweet water suitable for drinking. In the main these are surface rooting trees and the root course through the ground can be seen by a slight bulge on the ground surface, the roots lying from three to four inches beneath the soil. Roots from one- half inch to two inches diameter are suitable. To get clean water it is advisable to peel off the outer bark, break the roots in lengths'from 18 inches to three feet and stand them on end in a billy, noggin or bark dish. If the need for water is urgent, the root itself may be sucked, but it is advisable to peel back the first few inches of bark.

In arid or inland country the best water trees are Needle Bush, Mulga or Water Gums, Casuarina, Acacia and Currajong.

Needle Bush, usually 5 to 8ft. height. Although full- grown trees may reach 70 feet—one reported observer (Mr. Norman Lochhardt) says "the first root, about half an inch in diameter and six or eight feet long, yielded quickly and in large drops about a wine glass full of excellent water."

The "Red" Water Gums it is reported "always have water roots, gallons of water may be obtained ... a man is always safe as far as thirst is concerned with the Red Water Gum about him ... it is a permanent water supply." Another unknown observer remarked, "A quart-pot full of water was obtained in half an hour."

2.   WATER GUMS

Water Box in Western Australia is known by the aboriginal name of "Coolibah." Height up to 80 feet, extremely small fruit. Red Water Gum, called by many local names, bark smooth and from white to red in colour, seed vessel ribbed.

The Currajong of Central Australia is a dependable water tree; it is also known as the Bottle Tree, from the shape of its stem. The roots are very porous and con¬tain large quantities of drinkable water.

Desert Oak or She Oak (Casuarina) is a reliable water storage tree, one of its special features being cavities in forks or in the main trunk, into which rain water and dew trickles from the bark. These cavities are valuable reservoirs and should not be destroyed. They may be tested for water by inserting a stick into the small aperture and, if found to contain water, it may be withdrawn native fashion, by sucking through a tube of sections of bark or hollow grass stem. Another method is to wrap a piece of rag or dried grass or a stick to form a mop and, by immersing this in the water and squeezing it out in the container, a sufficient quantity of water may be withdrawn.

Acacias (Wattle Trees). Water cavities may occasionally be found in these trees. They are also water yielders in the roots; also many Acacias yield a water-containing gum which will relieve thirst.

3.   TO FIND WATER ROOTS

Generally the ground is dry and soft and, by probing into the earth with a pointed stick, the roots can be felt. With the stick lever up the root, break it off near the stem and then pull it right up to the end rootlets, break it into lengths and stand the lengths end on into a billy or dish – bark stripped from the biggest root section may be used as a gutter to drain the water into, in order to guide it into a pannikin, small noggin or a waterbottle.

In general, water is more plentiful from plants in gullies than from ridges. And the flow is quicker if the root sections are broken and not cut. Cutting with a blunted axe tends to bruise the capillaries and seal the moisture in the stems of the trees.

The stems of many young bush trees will yield a

small supply of water. This is a last resort. Young Gums, Stringybark and Angopheras have been so used.

4.   WATER YIELDING HERBAGE

Pig Face (Mesambryanthemum) yields a plentiful supply of moisture which can be obtained by mashing up or squashing the thick fleshy leaves and straining off the resulting fluid. The juice of Pig Face is reputed to be a good cure or preventative for scurvy. Pig Face is plentiful in many parts of the coastal and inland arid areas and can be recognised by the thick fleshy leaves. Ice Piant (Parakylia) also contains a great deal of moisture and is plentiful in many parts of the inland area. The method of obtaining water is similar to that recommended for Pig Face. The stems of many rock lilies are good water suppliers.

5.   WATER INDICATORS

Many birds and animals and insects will not travel far from fresh water and if these are seen in an area it is certain that water supplies are present. However, many animals and birds can travel long distances away from water supplies and therefore it seems advisable to know fairly accurately those creatures which are reliable indicators.

6.   FINCHES

The most dependable guides to water are the Finches, namely the Diamond Sparrow, Zebra Finch, Chestnut-eared Finch and Spotted Pardalots. From all over Aus¬tralia they are confirmed as an infallible sign in dry country of the near presence of drinking water, although the quantity may be only small. The traveller passing through the bush, should he come upon a small flock of any of these Finches, he will know he is close to water — careful watching will enable him to find it. The birds nest in root holes and in the banks of creeks.

7.   PIGEONS AND DOVES

All the Australian Pigeons and Doves are dependable water guides. Pigeons always live within reach of water and they range farther afield than the Finches. Their presence is an infallible indication that water is in the vicinity.

The unreliable birds include Crows, Kites, Eagles, Emus and Kookaburras. All these birds appear to be able to travel long distances from water. As a general rule the herbivorous birds are good water finders, while the insect and flesh-eating birds are unreliable indicators. Apparently the latter birds get sufficient moisture from the blood or juice of their prey.

8.   PARROTS AND COCKATOOS

These birds are not known to be reliable indicators of water in an area.

9.   HORNETS AND BEES

The Hornets and Mason Wasps and Bees are all reliable indicators of water. The Mason Wasp, really a long-legged, yellow-and-black wasp, paralyses its prey and builds it in the mud cavity where the egg is laid. If ever you see a Mason Wasp hover in the air over a special spot and then drop suddenly, you can be very sure of finding moisture, and by scratching or digging down you will find water.

Bees, also, and all the Hornet family will never live far from moisture — it may take some finding, but by watching the line of flight of the insect you will find the supply.

10.   ANIMALS

Dingo, Kangaroo and Wallaby tracks are not a reliable indication of the near presence of water in dry country. There may be water in the vicinity, but these animals are known to travel long distances between drinks. These tracks have often been seen several days' travel away from known water supplies. Cattle tracks are an indication of water in quantity and the animals invariably make well-defined pads to the source of supply.

11.   DEW

In many arid parts of Australia there are excessively heavy falls of dew. This may be collected by making mops of dried grass and squeezing the moisture into a container. A towel or cotton garment flopped among the herbage will quickly become wet enough to wring out, or large mops of dried grass tied around the ankles will collect water as one walks through the grass. Sandle-wood and many of the Acacias collect large quantities of dew, which can be collected by any of the methods outlined. Towels or garments laid overnight on stones out in the open will collect large quantities of dew.

12.   NATIVE WELLS AND STORAGE
RESERVOIRS

Throughout arid Australia there are native

wells and storage reservoirs. The general form in rocky country is in the form of rock holes; in other areas the water is found in the form of seepage holes or "soaks." The true native well is sunk in sand or soil, generally hidden beneath a bush and in a cluster of scrubby growth. The well itself frequently is curved inwards to protect the water from the sun and also from animals. At times the water in these native wells becomes badly polluted. (See water purifying)

13.   CREEK BEDS

Frequently water may be found below the surface of dry creek and river beds and by digging away the surface a soak can often be uncovered.

14.   SEA SHORE

All round the Australian coast fresh water springs are uncovered at low tide. These fresh water springs are generally near rock and the trickle of flowing water can be seen across the sand. A taste of the water on the finger tip will disclose whether the water is salt or sweet — if it is a sweet water flow a shallow soak hole just below the source will quickly fill up and prove a valuable reservoir.

15.   WATER FROM SEA FISH

The flesh of fish (sea) yields a clear, fresh-tasting fluid. The fish after it is caught may be cut up and either eaten raw and the fluid extracted by mastication, or alternatively the flesh may be cut up and placed in a piece of cloth which is folded over the fish pieces and squeezed, thus extracting the fish fluid in a fairly clear form. The same method may be used to extract drinking fluid from the flesh of birds or animals. The flesh of pippies, a triangular bivalve found on most surf beaches, is fairly fresh and not excessively salty, and will assuage thirst. The shells should be opened and the sand cleaned or washed out before eating.

16.   WATER PURIFYING

Water may be both muddy and infected – the muddiness can be removed, the water perfectly clarified, by applying a small quantity of powdered alum – this causes the mud to fioculate and it is precipitated. Water can be partly clarified by filtering through cloth of several thicknesses. If water is contaminated or polluted it may be decontaminated and made safe for drinking by either chlorinating with chloride of lime to give one part of free chlorine to one million parts of water – or more easily in the bush, simply boil the water for 10 to 12 minutes. It is advisable to do this with all water taken from dams where cattle drink, and from native reservoirs and rock beds. It is unnecessary to purify water obtained from root stems or tree holes, nor is it necessary to purify water which has been taken from streams flowing over sand or gravel. Generally water from soaks is pure.

CHAPTER 4
Edible Plants, Animals, Birds and Insects

1	*Edible plants, general.*
2	*Ferns.*
3	*Palms.*
4	*Grasses.*
5	*New Zealand spinach or saltbush.*
6	*Water cress.*
7	*Nettles.*
8	*Yams.*
9	*Taro.*
10	*Water lily roots.*
11	*Edible nuts —*
	Macadamia. Pandanus.
	Bunya. Coconut.
	Burrawong Palm Cones. Okari.
12	*Edible berries and fruits —*
	China Apple. Lilli Pilli.
	Wild Raspberry. Wild Grape.
13	*Edible birds.*
14	*Game.*
15	*Fresh water fishes and food —*
	Fishes.
	Yabbies.
16	*Saltwater fishes and food —*
	Crabs. Octopus.
	Shellfish. Poisonous Fish.
	Shark. Seaweeds.
	Turtle and Turtle Eggs.
17	*Edible insect foods —*
	Native Bees. Ants' Eggs.
	Wild Bees. Wood Grubs.

1.   EDIBLE PLANTS, GENERAL.

Edible plants, fish, animals and even insects are found throughout the whole Pacific area.

There are, however, some plants, and particularly fungi, which are extremely poisonous — there are also some forms of marine life which are dangerous to eat.

In the vegetable world a good general principle is to taste a small portion of the plant; if it irritates the skin of the lips, particularly the inside of the bottom lip, or the tongue, it is probably poisonous. In tropical areas avoid all fruits which are coloured red — red is the danger signal in tropical areas. With regard to fungi, the com¬mon mushroom and the young puff ball are both edible, but the unexperienced would be wise to avoid all the fungi.

Do not regard a plant as safe because you see birds, grubs or animals eating it. Many native birds and animals can eat berries and plants which would be fatal to man.

2.   FERNS

The young curls or fronds of bracken and other ferns, when they come up and are a few inches high through the ground are good food. They can be either eaten raw or lightly boiled; a billyful can be collected in a short time. Some ferns in fully developed leaf are poisonous, particularly when in spore.

3.   PALMS (See also Nuts and Fruits)

The heart or bud of many palms are both palatable and edible and may be either roasted or boiled. The removal of the heart kills the palm. The young fruiting corm of the Burrawong Palm is edible if

43

roasted, and it possibly may be boiled.

The central short tips inside the heart of the Xanthorrhoea (Grass Tree or Black Boy) are edible raw, or may be lightly boiled. They are quite palatable.

Bamboo shoots are edible and may be boiled.

4. GRASS TIPS

The underground shoots of Couch Grass, Buffalo and Kikuyu and all grasses are edible either boiled or raw — are quite palatable.

5. NEW ZEALAND SPINACH (TETRAGONIA)

This plant can be easily recognised by its light green leaves and yellow flower bracts. It is both palatable and edible either raw or boiled and fairly nutritious. It grows throughout the coastal belt of Australia and the islands.

6. WATERCRESS

Grows in most watercourses in the Pacific. May be eaten raw, but it is advisable to make sure the water supply where it grows is not contaminated. In the event of the water supply being contaminated, the water cress should be boiled.

7. STINGING NETTLES

Stinging Nettles but NOT the Nettle Tree are edible if boiled and quite palatable. Nettles are grown in France and eaten in place of spinach. When picking, grasp the nettle firmly or handle with gloves or hands wrapped up.

ROOT FOODS

Root foods in the main are an important source of starch or carbohydrates which rank very close to pure sugar as an energy producer. Almost all tubers must be cooked before being eaten.

8.   YAMS

Yams are vine growths found throughout Australia and the islands — the plant is distinguished by its long runners, having smallish dark green leaves that may be either oval or heart shaped (Sweet Potatoes belong to the Yam family) and the tubers may be either yellowish or purple as to the skin. Some Yams are acrid in taste and these should not be eaten until the acrid taste is washed out, which can be done by slicing the tuber across the grain and washing in water for an hour or so. Other Yams are fibrous and these should be grated or pounded before cooking or eating.

The identification of true Yams lies not in the tuber, but in the leaf which is distinguished by the branching of the veins which come from the base of the leaf and not from the midriff.

The tuber can be easily found by following the growth to the main point of entry into the ground and there digging down with a pointed stick or other implement until the main cluster of tubers is found. The tubers may vary in size from smaller in size than a man's fist to the size of a man's thigh. A cluster of Yams will provide food for many months.

After digging out the tubers, they should be tested and, if acrid or stringy, treated as mentioned.

They may be cooked by either baking or boiling and uneaten Yams may be cut into thin slices, placed on

45

flat stones in the sun and sun-dried for future use. Sun-dried or, more properly, de-hydrated Yam can be either powdered up or kept in slices and should be first soaked in water for a few hours, then lightly boiled or fried or made into cakes and baked.

Frequently Yams are affected by blight or disease and, unless the need for food is urgent, such diseased tubers are best left alone. They can be distinguished by brown streaks through the tuber. Yams are rarely found in open forest land. They generally grow in jungle or rain forest and like a rich soil and plenty of moisture.

9.   TARO

The Taro Plant is similar to an Arum Lily, the arrow- shaped green leaf having a purplish centre. The tubers can be either baked or boiled like English potatoes. Taro is not edible raw or half cooked.

10.   WATER LILY TUBERS

The fleshy tubers that are the roots of some species of Water Lilies are edible cooked. The Water Lily should not be confused with the Water Hyacinth, a purplish flower and fleshy green leaf that floats on the top of fresh water. The seeds of the Water Lily are eatable either raw or roasted. The leaf stems also are edible if peeled like celery, and the leaf after burning to an ash may be used to season food.

11.   EDIBLE NUTS

MACADAMIA OR QUEENSLAND NUT

Chief among the edible nuts is the Macadamia or Queensland Nut. The tree grows along watercourses and in gullies. The leaf is dark green, about 6 to 8 in. long, shallowly serrated, and the nuts, which are pale brown in colour and about 1in. in diameter, constitute one of the richest foods in the bush. The shell is exceptionally hard.

BUNYA PINE NUT

The ripe cone of nuts was looked on as a real prize by the Australian Aboriginal—the nuts may be roasted or baked and are rich in food value.

BURRAWONG PALM NUTS

These nuts, which are about 1 to 1 1/2 in. long, oval in shape, contain a kernel which is very palatable and nutritious after roasting. Cooking is essential. There have been cases of vomiting reported after eating this nut. It is always safe if the kernel is sliced and washed—the poison content is soluble in water.

PANDANUS

The Pandanus, which grows along the Northern Coast and throughout the islands, bears a nut which is a valuable source of food. The cone of nuts is fairly large, being from 6 to 10 in. in length and 4 to 6in. in diameter. In appearance it is like an inverted pineapple without the crest—on breaking the nut open, which requires some considerable force, there are a quantity of oval, greyish pods which surround the seed. The seed has a rich juice that has a decided scent of wine. These seeds are very oily and most nutritious. The outer containers must be cracked to obtain the seed which is securely locked inside. The young root tips are edible and very palatable.

COCONUT

The coconut and its edible qualities are too well known to require description.

OKARI NUT

This almond-flavoured nut grows plentifully in the New Guinea and island jungles. It is also found occasionally in the North Queensland scrubs. The nut and case itself is roughly lemon shaped, from 1 in. to 1 1/4 in. long, by from 3/4 in. to 1 in. diameter. It has a rough, fibrous husk which quickly decays. The fibrous husk is covered with a smooth dark brown case.

12.   BERRIES AND FRUITS

WILD RASPBERRY

The Wild Raspberry is similar to the Raspberry of cultivation and the fruit is borne on long canes and is bright red (usually a signal of danger) and slightly acid. It is edible, but not of high nutritional value. The wild raspberry is found in all rain forests or jungle areas of the Pacific.

CHINA APPLE

The fruit is a yellow to reddish sphere, shiny on the outside and about an inch or less in diameter. It grows on a thorny shrub with long vine-like canes. The fruit is palatable and edible. It can be found on all the North Queensland coastal area.

LILLI PILLI

The Lilli Pilli of New South Wales scrubs is edible. The fruit is purplish in colour with a hard seed inside. It may be eaten raw or cooked.

WILD GRAPE

This is one of the Lianas with a leaf made up of four to six oval-shaped leaves, somewhat like the leaf of the Virginia Creeper. The berries are deep purple, slightly acid, and edible.

GEEBUNG

This greenish coloured berry that grows in the N.S.W. coastal regions is edible and rather like a gooseberry in taste; it is excellent for jam making.

13. EDIBLE BIRDS

All birds are eatable, but not all are palatable. No birds are poisonous. The palatable birds include all the wild duck and geese, all the wild pigeons, doves, scrub hens, plain turkeys, hornbills (of North Queensland and the islands), and, of course, quail. Redbills, which are common in the swamps of the coastal areas, are palatable in stew, as are all the parrot family. Parrots, cockatoos and redbills are somewhat stringy and tough if baked.

The flesh of all birds can be dried into biltong.

14. GAME

All animals and reptiles are edible and none are poisonous, though some, like the wild pig, deer and rabbit, may contain eggs of, or worms, which can make man their host. For that reason the flesh should always be very well cooked before eating. For palatability and flavour the Red Fruit Bat (or Flying Fox), the Echidna or Spiny Ant Eater, and the tail and legs of the Goanna offer a surprise to the conventional eater of beef or mutton. It is a good general rule, if baking meat, and it looks stringy or tough, to wrap in clay, old news¬paper or banana leaves, and bury deep in the hot ashes for six to eight hours. Even tough shin of beef becomes a tender delicacy if cooked thus. Python, such as Carpet Snake or Diamond Snake, can be cooked into a delicious meal in clay, as can the Goanna.

If a large animal is killed or trapped, do not just cut off the flesh for one meal and leave the remainder to rot. Cut off all the edible flesh and smoke and sun-dry it into biltong. If you have no immediate use for it, hang it in a tree where it will be to some extent protected from the weather. It may serve you for food in 12 months time if you have put it beyond the reach of dingoes and foxes — or some other traveller near to starvation may find it.

15.   FRESH WATER FISHES AND FOOD

No fresh water fish are known to be poisonous and, as far as is known, all may be eaten, and all fresh water fish may be sun-dried. Fresh water fish may be trapped in the funnel mouth fish trap or by building simple fish weirs, into which the fish are driven. They may also be caught by line, either set lines or hand lines. Bait varies and includes the common earth worm, frogs, white wood grubs, grasshoppers, cicadas and flies of all types. Most fresh water fish will strike at a flashing spinner of tin, aluminium foil, white paper or red or white rag.

EELS

Eels are found in all fresh water streams east of the coast range, but not west, and are extremely rich. They may be caught with meat or any of the baits alluded to above or, if no hook is available, they may be allowed to completely swallow the bait and thus be slowly dragged ashore. Eel is best parboiled and then fried in its own fat.

The green frog is also edible, but the only portions worth eating are the hind legs, which may be grilled.

YABBIES OR FRESH WATER CRAYFISH

All yabbies or fresh water crayfish are both palatable and edible and highly nutritious. They may be caught by simply tying a piece of fresh meat to a piece of string and hanging it in the water. When the yabbies come to the meat, it may be slowly drawn towards the bank and the yabbie grabbed either with a pair of bush tongs or the hands. Yabbies have powerful nippers and can pinch. They are found in all fresh water courses, in rock pools and man-made dams and earth tanks, where they tunnel into the soil.

16.   SALT WATER FISHES AND FOOD

CRABS

All crabs living entirely on the land are reported poisonous. Most salt water crabs are edible and most are highly palatable after boiling, but be suspicious of brightly coloured salt water crabs. Crabs may be found all along the sea coast. Some are swimming crabs, some like open surf beaches, and others hide under kelp or seaweed; others clamber around rocks, others live in mangrove swamps and muddy estuaries, while others swim far out to sea; but if they are salt water crabs and not brightly coloured, they may be considered edible.

The swimming beach crabs may be found on the very edge of the surf. They bury in the sand as the wave washes back and will congregate toward any dead fish or other lure which is in the wash of the surf, and may be seen burying just as the wave washes back. They are easily scooped out with a quick movement of the hands to the dry sand above the wash, where they can be caught by holding down the back of the shell.

All the rock and kelp crabs can be speared, or caught with the hands in daylight, or at night when feeding they will freely come towards a bright light, and whole basketfuls may be caught by this means with ease.

The big blue crab of the mud flats and mangroves lives in burrows and may be pulled out with a loop of cane or lured out with a piece of meat, and thus caught. They, and lobsters, can also be caught in shallow flat nets lowered into the water, into which a bait is securely tied in the centre. Large crabs and lobsters can inflict a nasty wound . . . the crab with his nippers, the lobster with his tail, and both should be handled with respect. The hermit crab, which makes its home in a discarded shell, is also edible and can be caught in quantity in any rock-strewn pool.

SHELLFISH

The most commonly known edible shellfish include all the oyster family, all the clam family and pippies (a roughly triangular bivalve from one to three inches at the widest part, and found on nearly all surf beaches). The pippie washes about in the surf and, by extending a lip, can bury itself in the sand. They may be secured in large quantity by wading out at low tide and feeling down with the feet, where they will be felt in the sand like smooth stones. Any beach that has dead pippie shells washed up on it will have pippies. They live in colonies and prefer the short sand bars. It may take a while to find the colony, but when found it is valuable as a source of food supply. When taken from the sea pippies are full of sand and this should be washed from them before cooking. They may be eaten raw, or lightly boiled. The flesh is not excessively salty and will relieve thirst.

Salt water mussels, limpets, barnacles and periwinkles are all edible. In trying to describe the edible shellfish it must be borne in mind that different areas and localities have different varieties of marine life, most of which can be eaten with safety. Several types of shellfish are provided with protective poisonous spikes and, until these few types are recognised, shellfish of an unusual type should be handled with care. A good clue as to shellfish which are both palatable and edible can be found in studying the shell remains at any aboriginal midden in the vicinity. These middens or kitchens are all around the coast and contain a great variety of shells upon which the natives, in times past, feasted.

SHARK

All varieties of shark are edible, though not particularly palatable, except the gummy shark. Good steaks can be cut off the tail of the wobbegong or carpet shark.

STINGRAY

The flaps of the stingray are edible and may be boiled and cooked into a savoury and palatable meal.

OCTOPUS

The tentacles of the octopus found in rock pools are edible and quite palatable if boiled. The flavour is. like crab or lobster. The octopus is easily caught and can be lured with a smashed crab. It usually hides under rocky ledges and beneath flat stones.

SEA FISH

Some of the fish of tropical waters are poisonous as to the flesh and a general rule (to which there are many exceptions) is that any brightly coloured fish may be poisonous. Almost all dull coloured fish are edible, except the toads or bull routs. One or two fish have poison spines which can inflict painful or dangerous wounds. Of these the most dangerous is the stone fish, found in rock pools in the Barrier Reef. The stone fish is a sluggish lazy creature in appearance, not unlike a rock cod. It has a central spine with a poison duct and, if stabbed with the spine, the wound is fatal. The flesh is edible, but the carcase must be handled with great care. Many of the parrot fish of tropical waters have poisonous flesh, which will cause severe abdominal pains, vomiting and diarrhoea.

SEAWEED

Many of the seaweeds are edible if cooked by boiling. Experiment with local varieties is the best way to find out which are suitable. Some varieties contain an excessive quantity of iodine and would be unpalatable; apart from this, it is unlikely that any serious poison would result from any seaweed.

MARINE MAMMALS

All marine mammals, such as seals, porpoises, dugong, are edible.

TURTLES

Both the flesh of sea turtles and their eggs are eatable. The tracks are clearly seen after the tide and the scratchings in the sand where the eggs have been laid are easily found by following the tracks. The white part of the egg remains' watery after cooking, but may be eaten.

Some varieties of turtle can inflict a nasty wound with the beak, and another variety (Hawksbill) has a poison bag in the thorax. This should never be eaten. The flesh of this species and of all turtles is edible and can be cooked in steaks in the same manner as beef or mutton. The flesh may be smoked or sun-dried as for biltong.

17.   INSECTS

NATIVE BEES

Native bees are small, blackish, fly-like creatures which make their nest in a hollow stump. They have no sting. The honey, which is a valuable source of food, is dirty and should be strained. It is exceedingly sweet and from half a pint to a quart may be strained from a native bees' nest.

WILD BEES

These should not be confused with the native bees. Wild bees are the common English or Italian bees gone bush, and are not indigenous, as are the native bees. Wild bees' nests are very common throughout the scrubs and plains of Australia. The nest can be located by watching the bee's line of flight after it leaves water. This will take you directly to the bees' hive.

Wild bees in a district are a certain sign of water within a few miles. The honey is palatable and very rich in glucose. A man who is unconscious from exhaustion or starvation will revive in a matter of minutes if honey, sugar or glucose is given. It may be either administered in the mouth or in the rectum. Honey is probably the most precious and richest form of food in the bush.

WOOD GRUBS

The large white wood grubs found in rotten stumps and in tree roots are both palatable and nutritious. The blacks eat them raw — as we do oysters — but grilled they are more acceptable to the white man's palate. The flavour is like roast pork.

CHAPTER 5
Firelighting, Camp Accessories, Cooking and Tools

1	*Firelighting by friction drill.*
2	*Fire by flint and steel, and steel or pyrites.*
3	*Magnifying glass or mirror.*
4	*Splitting matches.*
5	*Firelighting, general.*
6	*Fireplace.*
7	*Noggin or water dish from tree bulb.*
8	*Slush lamp.*
9	*Camp oven.*
10	*Coolamin or bark dish.*
11	*Camp bed, ground pattern.*
12	*Camp mattress and camp loom.*
13	*Camp bed off ground.*
14	*Camp larder.*
15	*Camp table.*
16	*Camp gate.*
17	*Bush ladder.*
18	*Bush clothes peg.*
19	*Boiling water without a billy.*
20	*Baking without an oven.*
21	*Damper.*
22	*To preserve meat or fish by sun-drying.*
23	*Bush tools —*

Axe.   Bolo.
Tomahawk.   Cane Knife.
Machete.   Brush Knife.

24	*Knives from hack saw or file —*

Bowie.
Swedish.   Wood Splitting.

28	*General notes on cutting pegs and forked sticks.*

Fire may be obtained without matches, by friction as with the firedrill, by flint and steel, or by steel or iron pyrites, or by pieces of iron pyrites, or by means of either a magnifying glass or a concave mirror, focussing sunlight.

1.   FIREBOW AND DRILL

1.	Firebow —	Any bent bush stick.
2.	Head piece —	Any knotty piece of hardwood.
3.	Foot piece —	Lantana, beech, maple, spear of Xanthorrhoea, and many semi-soft native woods.
4.	Drill —	As above.
5.	Tinder —	Beaten grass, teased stringybark, very dry bark fibre, cotton or kapok fibre, etc.

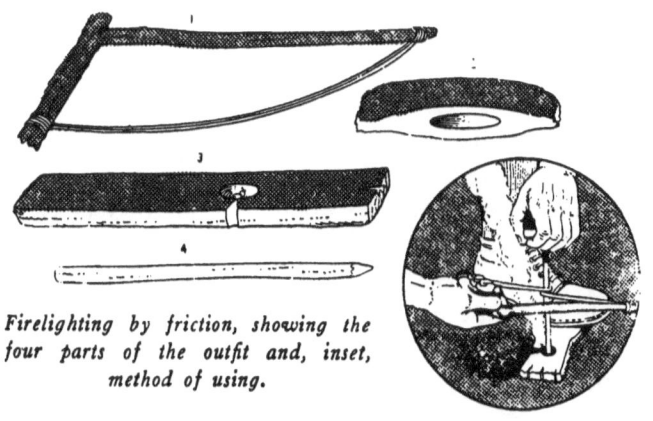

Firelighting by friction, showing the four parts of the outfit and, inset, method of using.

Bow rotates drill which is in hole in footpiece; leading into hole is a cleanly cut undercut V. Drill and footpiece grind out fine semi-burnt powder called "punk" which falls through V cut into tinder. Blowing on this punk will extend the spark and the tinder; blow¬ing the spark and the tinder together will cause the tinder to burst into flame. Practice alone makes perfect—flame has been got in 20 seconds.

2. FLINT AND STEEL OR IRON PYRITES

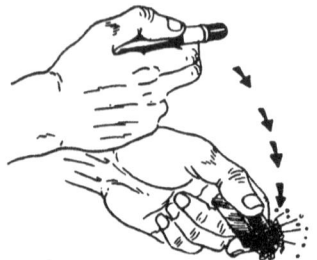

Position of flint steel and tinder.

The tinder is specially prepared, such as kapok fibre, scorched cotton or linen or very fine bark fibre, scorched and washed with finely ground charcoal and, if possible, nitre (saltpetre). A spark is struck which falls on to a pinch of the tinder and forms a glowing coal.

This is wrapped in teased out bark and fanned into flame.

3. MAGNIFYING GLASS OR CONCAVE MIRROR

The sun's rays are focussed on to dry teased bark, or other tinder. When it begins to smoke, blow the spark into flame. With skill and practice, it is said to be possible to shape a piece of ice between the palms of the hands into the form of a magnifying glass for fire-lighting.

4. SPLIT MATCHES

If matches are scarce, the match may be split and thus, with one match, it is possible to light two or three fires at different times.

To split the match, insert the point of a sharp knife or the point of a pin or needle immediately below the head. To strike the split match, keep the finger lightly pressed on the split head when striking it on the box.

5. TO LIGHT A FIRE

If after heavy rain, get the dry inside wood and split it up into fine twigs. Hold a bundle of these loosely in the hand and hold the match to them.

An alternative is to make a "fuzz" stick by paring back the outer wood from a dry stick. The pared back pieces are not cut off from the stick, but left sticking out. A match applied to them will cause the whole "fuzz" stick to catch fire.

If in early morning, break dry twigs off surrounding bushes. Do NOT get wood off the ground. Hold twigs in the hand and ignite with match.

Bark, paper or leaves, no matter how dry, are not always good for starting fire. They smoke and make too much ash and drown the prepared fire. It is always better to gather fine twigs.

6. FIREPLACE

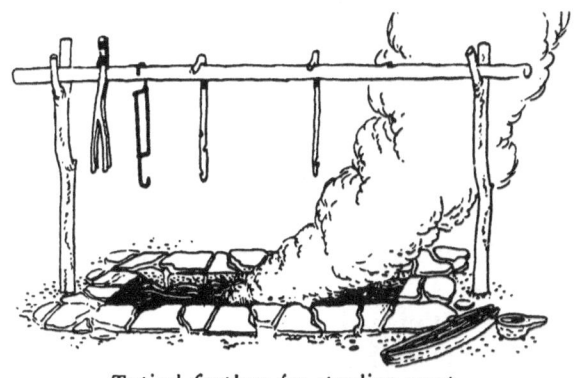

Typical fireplace for standing camp.

Place cross bar 3 to 4ft. above fireplace. Line the fireplace with stones, after first digging it out as a trench. NEVER use stones from a creek bed. They will explode.

Many other types of fireplaces will suggest themselves, depending upon the need of the moment. The only principle is that there will be a plentiful supply of air to the fire and that the fire itself cannot spread and start a bushfire.

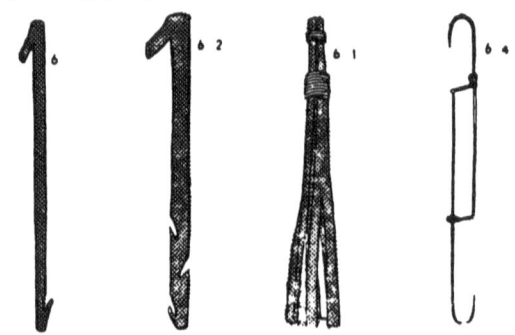

6 — (3) BILLY HOOK, with niche for billy. Simply an axe or knife cut bent back.

6 — (2) BILLY HOOK, with niche for billy handle cut back — two or three niches for adjusting length.

6 — (1) FIRE TONGS — One forked stick and one straight, lashed at end.

6 — (4) BILLY HOOK, wire, adjustable. The top link holds the adjustable portion secure at whatever height it is set.

7.   NOGGIN OR BOWL

Noggin or bowl for either storing liquid in, or for a mug. A — As it grows on the tree. B — Scarf cut in the tree. C — The finished noggin, hollowed out with a knife or burnt out with a stone, and either flattened at the bottom or with pegs to ensure it sits level.

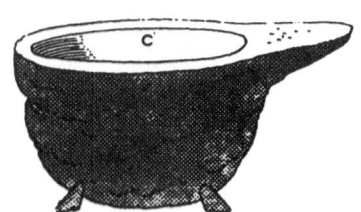

8. SLUSH LAMP

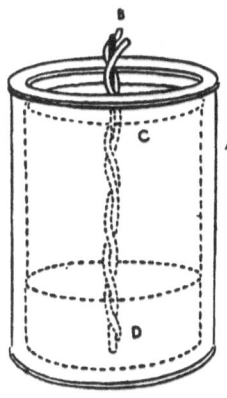

A — A tin, hollow piece of wood, section of bamboo.

B — Wick, fibre, piece of cotton rag, bark, etc., wound round a central stick, which is stuck into clay, D, at bottom.

C — Oil or fat. When lamp is lighted, fat is drawn up into wick. Extent of light depends on amount of wick.

9. COOLAMIN OR BARK DISH

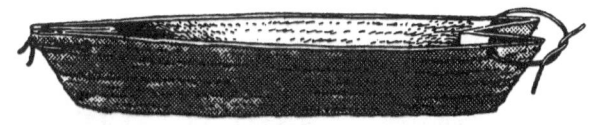

An opened cylinder of bark tied up at the end. Any smooth-flowing bark, such as Acacia, Stringybark, Ti-tree, etc. is suitable.

10. CAMP OVEN

Made from stones, plastered with clay and allowed to dry out; should be about 1ft. wide and about

1ft. 6in. high as a minimum—sides and wall about 6in. thick, with stone to cover front; fire is lighted inside and when it is thoroughly hot, fire is raked out and food to be baked is put in and stone put over door to keep in heat.

11.   CAMP BED ON GROUND

Camp bed and mattress, above.

Cut two poles, 5 to 6 in. diameter, and about 7 ft. long; drive in two pegs at head and feet, allowing about 2 ft. 6 in. between them—lay poles against pegs. Cut enough thick sticks to lay across poles for about 18 in. at head. Pack up space between poles with branches up to 1 in. thick. Lay on camp mattress.

12.   CAMP MATTRESS AND CAMP LOOM

Grass or fern is packed in and bar A is pulled down to ground, while warp tie B is passed between ties. Grass or fern is packed in between ties at A and top ties and A is lifted up and warp tie B is passed back between ties. After weaving ends are untied from end sticks, tied together, and mattress is ready

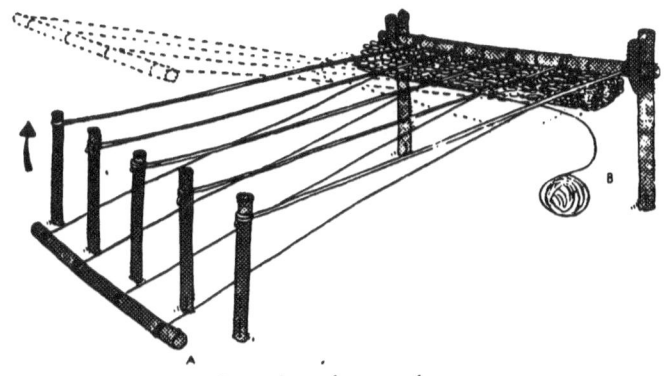

Camp loom for weaving.

13. CAMP BED OFF THE GROUND

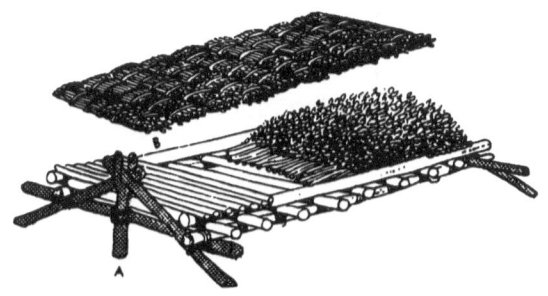

Raised camp bed with mattress, above.

Forked poles A, A should be driven into the ground and side poles leaned against forks; bed poles B, B can either support a chaff bag or have battens lashed across them for the bed. Camp mattress improves comfort, particularly if branches are used underneath, as on ground bed.

14. CAMP TABLE

Construction is the same as for a raised bed, but two additional cross bars are lashed below the table top; these cross bars project beyond the table edge and on to them a couple of saplings are laid for seats.

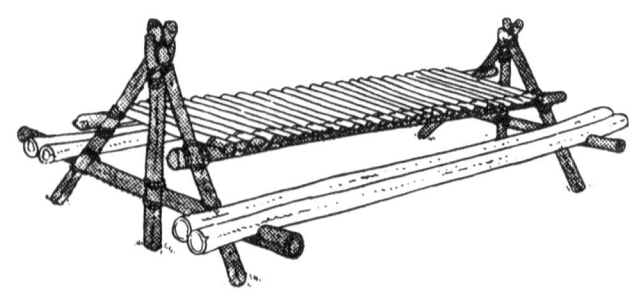

15.   CAMP LARDER

A small thatched structure is built about two or three feet above ground, and with a water tin or bucket sus¬pended above the roof; from this a few pieces of cotton rag hang to syphon water on to the top thatch. Evapora¬tion of water from the roof keeps the larder exceptionally cool. Air circulation is adequate if floor of larder is made as for camp table.

16.   CAMP GATE

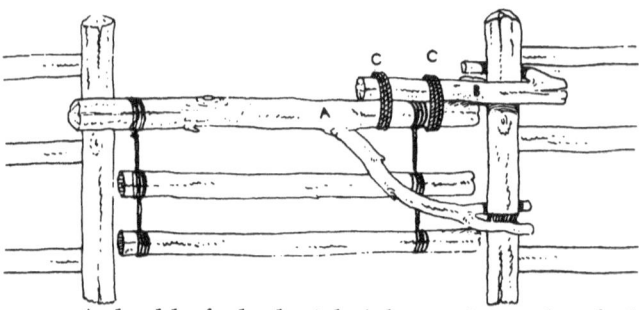

A doubly forked stick A has to it another fork B, lashed with sheer lashings at C, C; if desired, a collar or groove can be cut in the gate post
for the top and bottom forks.

17.   BUSH LADDER

Two long dry (if possible) poles lashed at top

with sheer lashings. Rungs are niched in to uprights and lashed' either with a square or diagonal lashing.

The triangular shape of the bush ladder is important for strength and rigidity. If the conventional shape of a house¬hold ladder is used, it will be unstable and have side play.

18.   CLOTHES PEGS

Take dry sticks about 6in. long — split with knife and cut away at entrance to split. Bind head with a simple sheer lashing.

CAMP COOKING

Apart from the ordinary cooking of stews, etc., which are well known, there are ways of cooking without equipment, and such cooking is in many instances an improvement as regards flavour on the civilized method.

19.   BOILING WATER WITHOUT A BILLY

Put your water in a coolamin, or scoop a hole in the ground and line with one piece of paper bark or, if no material is available for either coolamin or lining a hole in the ground, put water in your hat or tie up your trousers leg and put the water in there. Build up your fire and place in its centre a number of small stones, which will soon become white hot; lift these out of the fire with the fire tongs and drop in the water; in a few minutes the water will boil.

CAUTION. — Do not use stones from a creek bed. They will explode and may injure you.

20.   BAKING WITHOUT AN OVEN

Wrap up the meat or food to be baked in banana or palm leaves, damped newspaper, or in clay, and place deep in the ashes, not the coals, of the camp fire — in two or three hours you may remove the meat and it will be perfectly cooked; if left for longer periods, six to eight hours, it will not over-cook.

An alternative is to heat a number of large stones and line a pit or crater with them when they are red hot. Cover with banana or palm leaves and place food wrapped in banana, palm or other large leaves in the centre of the stones, cover with more leaves and top layer of sods or earth, and leave as if in ashes. Whole animals, such as wild pigs, are roasted in this manner.

21.   DAMPER

The conventional method of making damper with self- raising flour is too well known to need recital here. If you have plain flour and no raising, you can use the white ash of the wood, about 1 tablespoonful per lib. of flour — this is a soda ash and will serve as a rising. An alternative is to mix up flour and water into a paste and allow to ferment, mixing it after fermentation with the flour. Allow to stand, as for yeast, for an hour or so in a warm place till rising takes place. Bake as for bread in the camp oven or in the ashes.

It is a good tip to keep portion of the dough for the next baking. This is called sourdough.

22.   TO PRESERVE MEAT BY DRYING

Cut the meat into thin strips about 1in. thick by 1 to 2in. wide. Hang on a piece of wire or green stick so that no piece of meat touches another. Hang in smoke for 30 minutes to 1 hour, then hang in sun till quite dry. This meat is called biltong and will keep indefinitely. If the meat is very fat, it is advisable to cut off the fatty portion, as fat tends to go rancid. Flies will not blow the meat after it comes from the smoke. The outer surface must be dry. It may be hung in trees and will be quite edible. Eat raw or in stews after soaking in cold water for an hour or so.

CAUTION. — Do not use,eucalyptus leaves for smoke, or it will taint the meat.

FISH

Fish may be kept indefinitely by smoking for an hour and then breaking up in flakes and drying on hot stones placed in the sun. This sun-cured fish is quite palatable and may be eaten unprepared or boiled (after soaking) or made into fish balls. Eels, parboiled to remove some of the fat, and smoked and dried as fish, are also an excellent form of food.

23.   BUSH TOOLS

For bush work any of the following tools are satisfactory: —

Axe	Tomahawk.
Machete.	Bolo.
Cane Knife.	Brush Hook.

These tools are quite inefficient unless kept razor-sharp. A good bushman will always have his axe so sharp that he can cut his bread and sharpen his pencil with it.

An axe or tomahawk with a shoulder to its edge is definitely dangerous. There will surely come the chance blow on the edge of a cut which causes the head to glance off and the result may be a badly gashed foot or leg. Always keep the shoulder ground off an axe edge, and never put an axe in the ground. Always sink it in a tree butt or stump. To keep a tool sharp the best stone is a small circular carborundum, coarse on one side, fine on the other. There is no need to use oil—a drop of water or a good spit will do quite nicely to bring up the edge.

24. KNIVES

A very satisfactory bush knife can be made from a machine hack saw blade, broken off to about 10 or 12 inches and ground off on the back of the hack saw blade, leaving the saw edge for the back of the knife. If you are grinding off the saw blade on a power grinding wheel, be careful not to burn the steel. By leaving the saw edge on the back of the knife you have a most efficient tool for sawing through small saplings and light timber. A hack saw knife is brittle and should never be used as a lever or it will snap off.

The handle may be of wood or bone or horn and can be riveted through the hole in the end of the saw blade and wire bound at the base of the handle.

A very good heavy knife can also be made by grinding down an old file.

25. BOWIE KNIFE

A good bowie knife is worth carrying, but make sure it has good steel and guard its edge.

26. SWEDISH KNIFE

This type of folding knife, made by Holmberg, of Sweden, is recommended as the best of the bush knives for general purposes. They are very safe, the blade cannot fold back, the steel is good, and they are light to carry.

27. WOOD SPLITTING

For splitting wood never bury your axe up to the head in a new split. It is far easier to sharpen up a few hardwood wedges, ironbark for preference, and keep driving them in as the crack opens up, using the head of the axe for driving, and cutting the cross grain of the timber with the axe, rather than use it as a wedge.

28. GENERAL NOTE ON PEGS AND FORKS

Always bevel off the head of a peg and sharpen well, so that it will drive easily. Dry pegs drive more easily and are less liable to split than green pegs.

In selecting fork sticks that are to be driven into the ground, always select a stick that has the fork branching off the main stick rather than one in which the main stick divides. By selecting a fork as recommended, you can drive on the main stick and will not split off the fork.

CHAPTER 6
Water Travel

1   *Rafts.*

2   *Bark canoes.*

3   *Coracle from tent fly,*

4   *Balloons in ration bags.*

5   *Ground sheets bolstered.*

6   *Trousers or shirt inflated.*

7   *Pole for non-swimmers.*

8   *Bridging,*

9   *To measure the height of a tree.*

10   *To measure the width of a stream.*

Water travel may be improvised in various ways, depending upon the material available, the water to be travelled and the number of people or equipment to be moved.

1.   RAFTS

The easiest method for construction, if material is available, is the raft. A number of light poles (bamboo is eminently suitable) are lashed together and on to cross pieces until the area built up is sufficient to float the load. There is little in the construction of a raft other than common sense. If travelling down broken fast water it is advisable to have for a kellick a large stone or hard wood log astern, so that it can be dragged along the bed of the stream and so reduce the speed that the raft can be steered from the forward end.

2.   CANOES

Quite a serviceable canoe can be made from either green ironbark or stringy bark.

The tree is selected from which the cylinder of bark is to be stripped. It must be a straight trunk, free from branches, and the bark must lift freely (it is well to test the tree for this before stripping). The bark is cut through a foot or so above the butt and at the height required (which equals the length of what will be the canoe). These two ring bark cuts are then joined by a third cut along the entire length of the trunk and these vertical edges eased off the trunk by the axe. Into the eased off edges two flattened

71

saplings are inserted and, by working them up and down along the vertical edges, the whole cylinder of bark can be taken off in one piece without a crack or break.

The rough dry outer bark is pulled off and the cylinder of cleaned bark is stood upright and a quick fire lighted in the bottom end. After a few minutes the sap will have steamed through the last few feet of the end and the cylinder is now upended and the processes repeated upon the other end.

Steaming the cylinder of bark.

Alternative is to lie the cylinder of bark horizontally on the ground and light a quick fire of dry leaves and small twigs throughout the length of the cylinder.

The action of the fire is to drive the sap through the bark and make it more pliable (in much the same way that a plank of timber is steamed), so that it can be bent without breaking it. The cylinder of bark may be gently and slowly turned inside out. (If for any reason it shows signs of splitting at the end it is advisable not to turn it.) With a sharp knife, holes are cut in the two sides of each end, as per sketch.

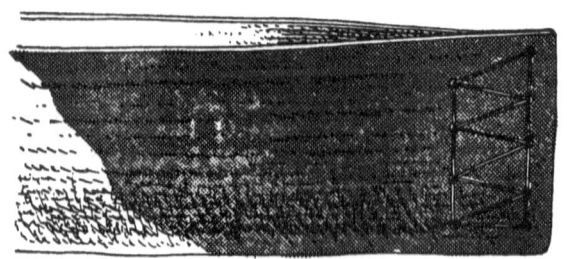

Showing method of sewing the ends of canoe.

72

Through these holes thongs for lacing the ends together are passed. These thongs may be strips of stringy bark from the inner layers, teased and laid together into strong cords, or they may be vines or other suitable very strong materials. The lacing is pulled tight and secured and the joined edges of the bark cylinder beyond the lacing are neatly trimmed with a sharp axe or knife. The inside of the lacing is packed with well puddled clay and the canoe is now ready for the spreaders.

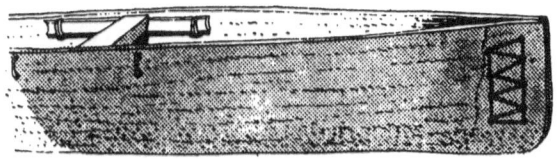

Spreaders and spreader bars are in position.

Six or seven feet from the ends of the canoe, four holes are cut, about 5in. apart vertically and about 2ft. horizontally. A bar, into which the spreader fits, is lashed through these holes as indicated by the sketch and the canoe gently pulled apart to allow the spreader to drop into slits previously cut in the centre.

The spreader's weight is thrust against the spreader bars and distributed over some of the length of the canoe instead of directly against the bark. These bark canoes are quite strong and seaworthy and will last quite a long time if kept in the water—removed from the water for any length of time the bark cracks and the canoe is no longer very serviceable.

Paddles may be improvised from light dry split wood. A bark canoe of 20ft., with 3ft. to 4ft. spread, will safely take a load of six to eight men and gear. The measurements for two men would be 10ft. to lift., and 3ft. to 3ft. 6in. spread.

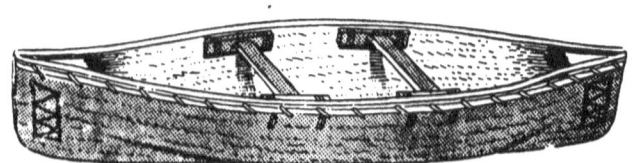

The finished bark canoe with strengthening gunwale strip sewn around the top.

3. CORACLE

A coracle for deep water travel may be improvised from a tent fly and bush timber.

Drive a double row of stakes in the ground, about 8in. to 10in. apart, in a roughly oval shape, that is, about three-quarters the length of the fly, and three-quarters the width.

The framework for the coracle is being built up with brushwood placed between stakes driven into the ground.

In between these double rows of stakes, pile young branches from green saplings, using sticks up to 1in. in thickness. Now bind the branches together with stringy bark cord, vine or other suitable material, making a light oval framework, about 2ft. high, and with sides about 6 to 8in. thick. Across the bottom of this framework a cross section is lashed and the whole is laid lengthways on the fly, which is now folded over the outside and down on the inside, tucked under or tied to the bottom of the framework. If the coracle is very long and wide, a spreader can be put in, very much after the style of spreader used in the native canoe.

Framework of brush-wood for the coracle completed and removed from the stakes.

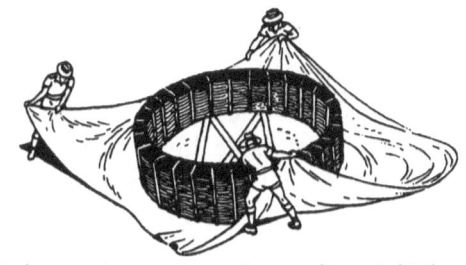

Placing the framework on the tent fly and folding the fly over.

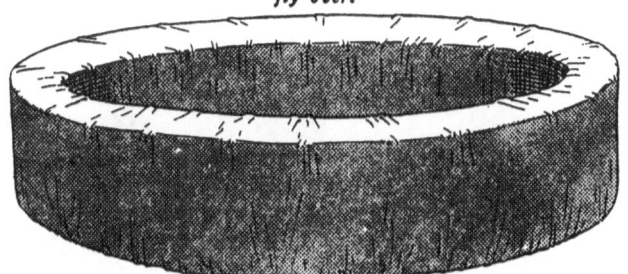

The finished coracle, about 11ft. long by 8ft. wide by 2ft. deep.

These coracles are quite seaworthy and will support a heavy load and can safely be used in light surf and not too heavily broken water. They also provide an easy means of river travel if there are not too many snags.

Water travel without special gear can be improvised by several means.

4. BALLOONS IN RATION BAGS

A trip was made by one party who inflated toy balloons inside ration bags and used them as water wings. Ground-sheets supported their packs. The method proved completely satisfactory.

5. GROUND SHEETS

The ground sheet is laid flat in the ground and a bolster of branches is placed lengthways along the centre; ends of the ground sheet are folded upwards and inwards and the sides rolled over to over-lap. Two or three of the bolsters can be lashed on to a pole, top side uppermost, and this light improvised raft will easily support two men. The bolster should be about 4ft. long and about 1ft. in diameter.

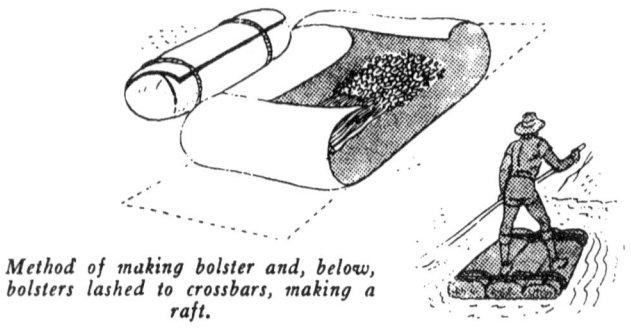

Method of making bolster and, below, bolsters lashed to crossbars, making a raft.

6. TROUSERS INFLATED

By removing the trousers and either tying up the end of the leg or knotting the end of the leg with a thumb knot and inflating the trousers with air, by swinging them over the head, they can be made to support a man in the water for several hours. The crutch is placed under the chest and the two legs allowed to pass under the arms like water wings. With practice the trousers can be removed in the water and inflated by swinging over the head and down while the operator treads water. Shirt sleeves inflated and tied or knotted can also be used to support a man in the water by exactly the same method as is used with the trousers.

If the garments are first wetted they will keep you afloat longer. They may be easily re-inflated in the water.

7.   POLE

By grasping the base of a light bamboo pole firmly between the ankles and the knees and "riding" it, a non-swimmer can safely negotiate deep water streams. The pole leans forward about 45 deg. from the swimmer, who paddles with his hands for forward motion. This takes very little practice and is a most useful method for all occasions for crossing streams and narrow portions of a deep river.

8.   BRIDGING

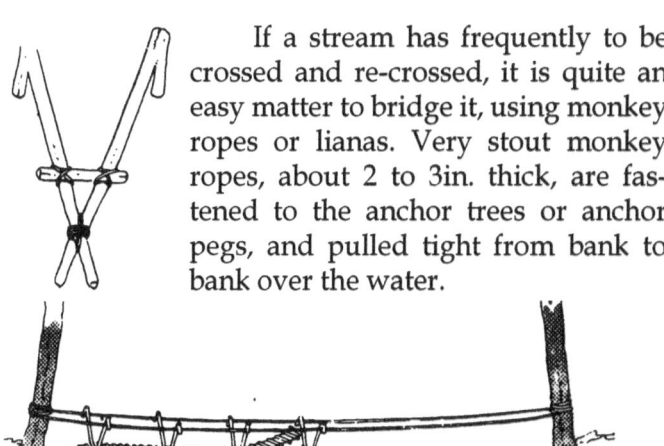

If a stream has frequently to be crossed and re-crossed, it is quite an easy matter to bridge it, using monkey ropes or lianas. Very stout monkey ropes, about 2 to 3in. thick, are fastened to the anchor trees or anchor pegs, and pulled tight from bank to bank over the water.

Showing how frames are pushed out along ropes and decking sections dropped on to crossbars.

Inverted "A" frames, as per sketch, from forked sticks are pushed out from the nearer bank and the section of decking is dropped from the nearer bank on to the cross bar of the frame ("A") (The section of decking is simply small sticks of 1 to 2in. diameter lashed to two saplings.)

From this first section of decking the next y frame is pushed out on the side ropes and the next section of decking is dropped on to it—and so on until the bridging is completed.

An alternative to the inverted "A" frame is a monkey rope loop pushed out along the side ropes. If no anchor trees are available, anchor can be made by driving in three pegs, and in front of these two pegs, and in front again one stout peg. The ropes are secured to the first peg, which is lashed back to the two pegs, which in turn are lashed back to the three pegs. This anchor will take almost any strain.

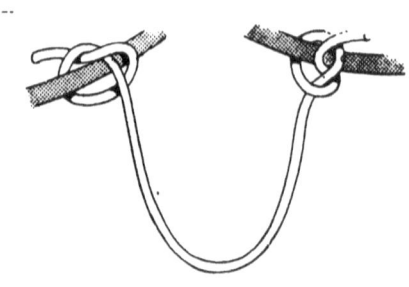

If it is found that the side ropes are too close a spreader can be put between them at either end. If the bridge has a big span or has much side sway, a third thick monkey rope may be passed below the bottom crossing of the inverted "A" frame and pulled tight on either bank.

9. TO MEASURE THE HEIGHT OF A TREE OR A CLIFF

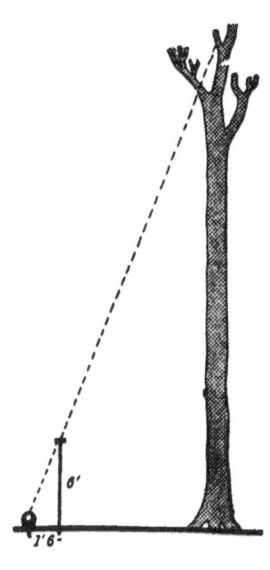

Cut a stick of known length, say 6ft. stick. Put the stick up-right in the ground some dis¬tance away from the height to be measured. Get the eye to the ground and keep moving away from the stick until the top of the stick and the height of the tree are in line, and measure the distance from the eye to the base of the stick. Say it is 1ft. 6in. — therefore every 1ft. 6in. in distance from the eye to the base of the tree will repre¬sent 6ft. (or the height of the stick). Thus if the distance from the eye to the tree in this example is 10 feet —

$$\frac{10}{1\frac{1}{2}} = 6\frac{2}{3}, \text{ which is } 6\frac{2}{3} \times 6 = 40\text{ft.}$$

10. TO MEASURE THE WIDTH OF A STREAM

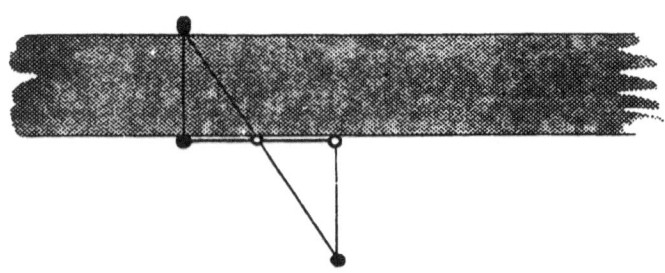

Select some prominent object on the far side of the stream directly opposite to where you stand. Put a stake in the bank at your position — move at right angles for a known number of paces (say 5), and put another stake in the ground. Continue for an equal number of paces (5) and place another stake upright in the ground. Now turn at right angles and move in from the stream until the prominent object on far bank of the river, the centre stake, and you, are in line. If you measure the distance from your position to the last of the three stakes it will equal the distance across the river.

CHAPTER 7
Direction Finding and Time

1   *To get north from sun and watch.*

2   *To get north from stick.*

3   *To get north with a plumb bob.*

4   *North from stars.*

5   *South from Southern Cross.*

6   *South from Magellan Clouds.*

7   *South from Canopus and Achernar.*

8   *Time from Southern Cross.*

9   *Instructions for sun compass.*

10   *Sun compass to mount on metal or paper.*

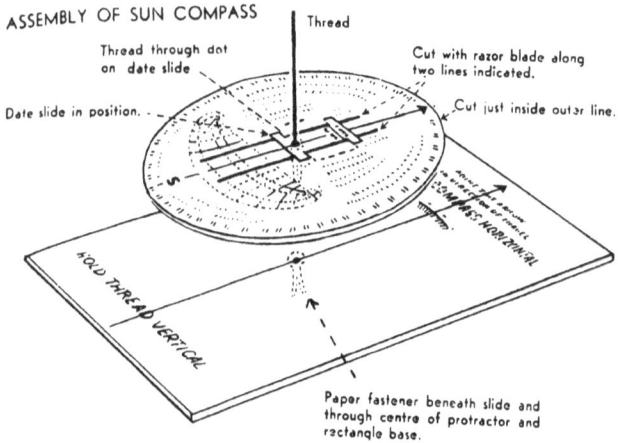

ASSEMBLY OF SUN COMPASS

Thread

Thread through dot on date slide

Cut with razor blade along two lines indicated.

Date slide in position.

Cut just inside outer line.

S

COMPASS HORIZONTAL

HOLD THREAD VERTICAL

Paper fastener beneath slide and through centre of protractor and rectangle base.

Sun Compass assembled and in use—see page 82.

DIRECTION FINDING IN THE BUSH

Direction in the bush can always be found either from the sun or from the stars; in addition time, to within thirty minutes, can be obtained after practice from the Southern Cross.

1. TO GET APPROXIMATE NORTH FROM THE SUN BY WATCH

If south of the equator, point 12 o'clock of your watch to the sun and halve the distance between the hour hand and the 12 o'clock position.

If north of the equator point the hour hand to the sun and halve the distance between the hour hand and 12 o'clock on the watch dial.

This is approximate only. If you are working on daylight saving time, make the necessary hour allowance on the hour hand.

2. TO GET ACCURATE NORTH FROM THE SUN WITH A STICK

Put a stick upright in the ground shortly before mid¬day. Where the shadow of the head of the stick touches the ground place a twig—every ten or fifteen minutes record the shadow of the head of the stick with twigs until the shadow has shortened and commenced to lengthen. Connect up the arc formed by the twigs and measure from the base of the stick to the closest point of arc. An extension of this line will give you true north accurately. Alternatively plumb method (3) may be used with the stick.

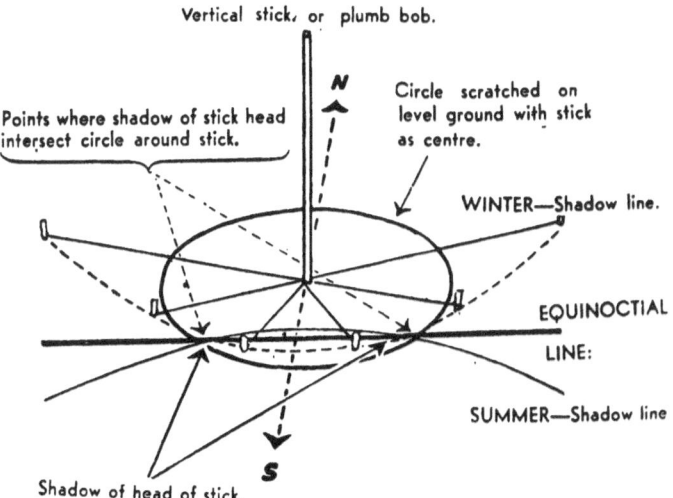

Vertical stick, or plumb bob.

N

Points where shadow of stick head intersect circle around stick.

Circle scratched on level ground with stick as centre.

WINTER—Shadow line.

EQUINOCTIAL LINE:

SUMMER—Shadow line

S

Shadow of head of stick.

NOTE.—If you are north of the Tropic of Capricorn and the sun is south of the equator, the sun shadow may be north of your stick.

The sun shadow stick method may be done accurately about the period of the Equinox (March and October) by getting two points of shadow at about ten to twenty minutes' interval at any time of the day. These two points connected are accurately east and west and any right angle from them is north and south.

3. PLUMB BOB

A plumb bob with a stick or bulb some feet off the ground and the weight just touching the ground; from the centre where the plumb bob just touches the ground draw an arc so that the shadow of the bulb will cut the arc. Set pegs as before and complete the arc of sun shadows; from the points where the original arc from the plumb bob intersects the arc of the shadow, draw a line on the ground and accurately bisect it — extend a line from the bottom of the plumb bob to the bisected point and extend this. This is an accurate north-south line.

4. DIRECTION FROM THE STARS

North in the Northern Hemisphere may always be found from Polaris, which is over the North Pole.

5. SOUTH FROM SOUTHERN CROSS

The Southern Cross may be seen in the Milky Way and can be easily found by the Coal Sack (a dark area) which lies alongside the Cross. It can be identified by the two pointers.

The longest length of the Cross from the head (Gamana Crucis) towards the foot (Alpha Crucis), if extended four and a half times, brings you to a point directly over the South Pole. A line dropped from this point to the horizon will give south accurately.

There is no bright star over the South Pole.

6. MAGELLAN CLOUDS

On moonless nights two masses of nebulous cloud may be seen below the Southern Cross. These are called the Magellan Clouds and, if viewed as the base of an equilateral triangle, and the apex visualized, then the apex is over the South Pole, and a line dropped from this point to the horizon will be true south.

7. CANOPUS AND ACHERNAR

If in northern parts of Australia and in the Pacific Islands, there are times when the Southern Cross is below the horizon. At such times true south can be found by identifying Achernar and Canopus. Achernar is a bright star lying about nine times the length of the Cross towards the foot, and Canopus is a bright star, about midway between the bottom star of the Cross (Alpha Crucis) and Achernar, and equidistant from the Celestial South Pole (four and a half times from the foot of the Cross).

Canopus and Achernar are the base of an equilateral triangle of which the apex is the Celestial South Pole. Drop a line from this imaginary point in the sky to the horizon and you have the true south.

NOTE. — If you are interested in this work of direction finding, the hand book, "Elementary Astronomy" issued by the Sydney Observatory, Sydney, is recommended for its usefulness and valuable information; also recommended is "Direction Finding," by Dr. F. S. Woolnough.

8. TIME BY SOUTHERN CROSS

To find time by the Southern Cross within 30 minutes:

(a) Take the extended arm of the Southern Cross as the hour hand of a clock — the clock face being an imaginary circle formed by rotating the extended arm of the Cross round the point where the arm and the perpendicular line to the horizon cut, as per diagram.

85

(b)   Divide the clock face into 24 equal parts representing 24 hours instead of the usual 12. Therefore, reading the hour hand in the diagram above, it is pointing to 19.15 hours.

(c)   To find the time from this point add two hours for each month to the next March 31st. For example: If the above diagram represented the position of the Southern Cross at any time on the night of April 15th, 1942, one hour would be added for the half of April, and two hours for each full month up to 31st March, 1943, which makes a total of 23 hours.

Hence the time would be 19.15 + 23 = 42.15 hours, or 42.15 − 24 = 18.15 hours (midnight is 24.00 hours).

The important things to remember are: —
(a) Accuracy in reading the clock face in the sky.
(b) To allow for the unexpired portion of the month in which you are working.

To find Southern Cross, look along the Milky Way. The Cross is near a dark patch called the Coal Sack.

Always recognize the Southern Cross by the pointers.

SUN COMPASS

ASSEMBLY

The Sun Compass, as applied for bush work, consists of three parts: —
Base.
Protractor and Time Plate.
Date Slide.

To assemble, cut out the three components, mount on celluloid or cardboard or thin metal, and secure pro¬tractor to base with a flat-headed paper fastener, passing exactly through the centre of each.

Through the small hole at one end of date slide pass a thick thread and knot on the back. Slip in the date slide with the thread end towards the time plate.

USES

The Sun Compass will give you accurately any of these three factors: —
  True north.
  Accurate solar time (to within two minutes).
  Any required bearing.

It is desirable to know one of these factors to obtain the other two. For instance, if time is known, true north or any bearing can be easily obtained; conversely, if any bearing is known, time and true north can be obtained; or, if true north is known, any bearing and time can be obtained.

HOW TO USE

1.   IF TRUE NORTH IS KNOWN

Point the arrow of protractor to true north. Move date slide till date line opposite approximate date. Hold thread taut and quite vertical and protractor quite horizontal. Read off along shadow of thread the time (see 2), which is where the thread shadow intersects the line of your latitude (latitude lines are the oval dotted lines). Time is shown by the cross lines.

The arrow of the base points the direction of which you want the bearing. Read off the bearing between arrow of protractor and arrow of base.

2.   HOW TO USE WITH WATCH

If time is known by your watch it will be standard time (which is "average" time on a given meridian of longitude). You must adjust your watch to solar or sun time on the longitude where you are working.

The figures opposite the dates represent the number of minutes standard time is ahead or behind solar or sun time. If minus, take off the indicated number of minutes from your watch. If plus, put on the time to your watch.

There is one other adjustment to your time, and that is to correct it for your longitude. If you are east of the longitude on which standard time is taken, the sun is ahead of standard time. Therefore put your watch on four minutes for each degree east. If you are west, the sun is behind standard time, therefore put your watch back four minutes for each degree west that you are.

Having now corrected your watch to solar time for the longitude you are in, and set the date slide, hold the thread vertical and the Sun Compass level, and turn circular protractor until the thread shadow crosses the corrected time on the time plate. The arrow of the time plate will now be pointing true north and the bear¬ing will again be the difference between arrow of base and true north of protractor.

3.   WHEN A BEARING IS KNOWN

Set the bearing on the protractor against direction arrow of base plate. Therefore north line of protractor is pointing to true north, and by pulling thread taut and vertical, after setting date slide, and holding the Sun Compass level, the point of intersection of the shadow with the correct latitude line will accurately indicate solar time (see 2).

4.   HOW TO USE AT NIGHT

Discover true south; and point the REVERSE (south) end of the protractor to the south. The direction arrow or base will show the bearing required if read as for 1 or 3. For night use the thread and slide are not used. Alternatively in the Northern Hemisphere, point the north of protractor towards the Pole Star.

POINT THIS ARROW
IN DIRECTION OF TRAVEL
HOLD COMPASS HORIZONTAL

Cut.

HOLD THREAD VERTICAL

ASSEMBLY OF SUN COMPASS

Cut just inside outer line.
Cut with razor blade along two lines indicated.

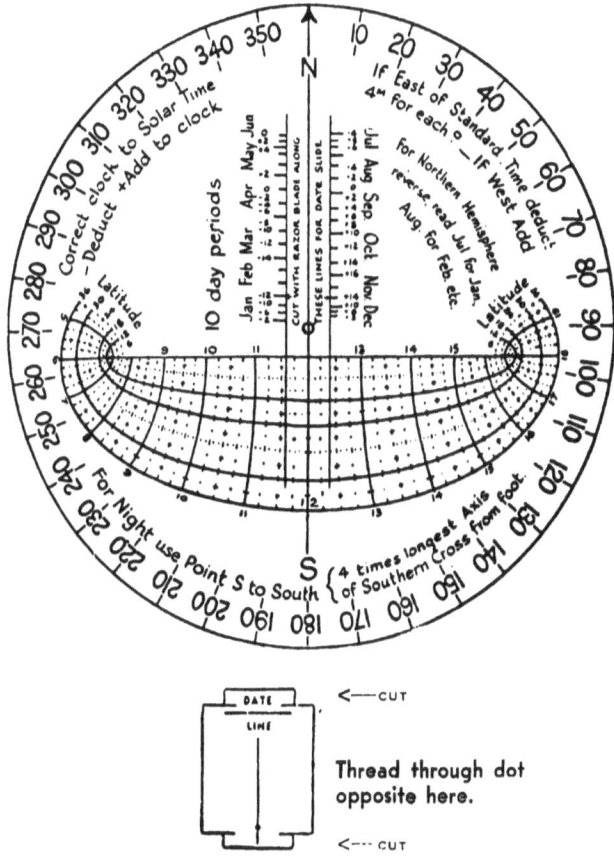

Thread through dot
opposite here.

93